BODY MOVEMENT
FOR
CHILDREN

An Introduction to Movement Study and Teaching
by
MARION NORTH

Publishers   PLAYS, INC.   Boston

Copyright © 1971 by Macdonald & Evans Ltd.

Published in Great Britain under the title
An Introduction to Movement Study and Teaching
This book is copyright and may not be reproduced in whole or *in part* (except for purposes of review) without the express permission of the publisher in writing.

First American edition published by
Plays, Inc. 1972

Library of Congress Catalog Card Number: 70-184230
ISBN: 0-8238-0132-2

PRINTED IN GREAT BRITAIN

PREFACE

The suggestions which are made in this guide are the result of experience in working practically with children, teachers, students and adult groups. It is intended that any teacher could use this guide, even without much personal practical experience – this could be gained alongside teaching the children. I have, therefore, avoided using a great deal of technical terminology. The overriding idea in this book is to show how movement can be observed in everyday life, and how it relates to ideas and material for teaching movement to young children. The ideas described are based on the research into the knowledge of the principles of movement as expounded by Rudolf Laban. The practical application of these ideas in England was first developed by Lisa Ullmann at the Laban Art of Movement Centre. My thanks and appreciation are to both Mr. Laban and Miss Ullmann, with whom I worked for many years. I am also grateful to Miss Mary Seyd, who supplied the drawings.

M.N.

CONTENTS

	Preface	iii
	Introduction	v
1	The body is the instrument	1
2	The movements of the body have different accents and stress	8
3	Activity and recovery	16
4	The body moves into different zones of space	26
5	Stopping the flow of movement resulting in different shapes of the body	35
6	The balance of the weight of the body	51
7	The body draws shapes in the surrounding space	54
8	The lesson	59
9	Using percussion instruments	66
10	Action images taken from nature	74
11	Group movement: relationships with others	82
12	Movement, colour and pattern	93

INTRODUCTION

THE study of human movement in Western culture is probably in its infancy, and its full development lies in the future. No doubt some years hence there will be a department of movement in every university, and it will be recognised that the scope of the subject is as broad as that of any other discipline at present studied. There are as many applications of movement knowledge as there are applications of, for instance, psychology. These include the Arts (not only dancing, drama and music but the visual and so-called static arts, architecture, painting, modelling, etc.); the understanding and treatment of maladjustment; the education of children and adults; and the practical affairs of daily life in, for instance, industry and commerce. Reports and publications are just becoming available of practical work in these spheres – work which has been developed over the past twenty to thirty years in the U.K., the U.S.A. and Canada.

This introduction aims to discuss the place of movement in education, and, although I have practical experience in other spheres, I write as an educationalist who has found that movement is a valuable medium through which children and adults can be helped in their growth and development.

Ideas about what movement education is vary so much even among its exponents working in schools and colleges that it is not surprising to find colleagues in other disciplines ranging in their attitudes towards the subject from great enthusiasm to sceptical indifference. The range and variety of work in movement education, developed over the last twenty years, is both the strength and weakness of the subject: strength because of the vitality and richness of activity, weakness because some of the work which can be seen under the guise of "movement" shows misunderstanding of its most significant aspects and, therefore, should probably never be inflicted upon children or adults. But this can also be said of many other subjects taught in schools, and the contribution of movement to education should not be assessed on the basis of the least understanding of its exponents.

Perhaps I could start by saying what I think movement education is *not*. It is not physical education, though many aspects of movement understanding and practice have been incorporated in some physical education programmes to the great enrichment of the work. It is not dancing (in the sense of learning set dance forms, or in the sense of spontaneous "prancing about"), although the art form of dance is a facet of movement education which can greatly contribute to an education programme by formulating movement expression. In the same way those artistic activities in the dramatic sphere where movement is either an integral part, or even perhaps the starting point or main activity (*i.e.*, dance-drama or mime and caricature), are not *in themselves* movement education. And, although it has been used in connection with personality assessment, movement is not a science in which personality can be measured, tabulated and compared statistically with other tests of personality traits – though again, there are clearly defined areas of movement which can be differentiated, described and to some extent measured. (It is, however, probably more accurate to say "assessed" rather than measured, except in those obvious areas like the number of times a particular movement is repeated, or the measurable length of time taken, or the amount of muscular energy expended and so on.) I should probably also state quite clearly that real movement education has nothing to do with the vague floating about in space to some external music or sound, which unhappily can still be seen in some educational establishments. And it should be remembered that the now almost traditional *Music and Movement* broadcast programmes were originally created to help the young child to appreciate *music*, and no claim is made by the producers of these programmes that a movement education is being given.

Introduction

It is manifestly impossible to teach children in the realm of movement (which after all should be through the experience of movement patterns, rhythms and sensations) when the broadcaster cannot see the response and relate the subsequent task to the needs of the children. Some stimulation can indeed be given, but the real educational activity, which is the development of that initial response, cannot be incorporated even if the teacher on the spot tries to do a "follow-up" programme – the subtlety of timing, intuitive response and using of the material of the moment which all good teachers have, are completely lacking. Some teachers have taped the lessons, and used parts of them quite cleverly to enrich their own ideas. Usually this is a stage of development for the teacher, and is often dropped after the usefulness – a "prop" for the less confident teacher – has passed. There could well be a place for a real contribution to movement education through the television medium, which I will discuss later.

Finally, I should say that movement education like, for instance, music, art, craft or poetry, is not dependent upon the ideas of any one person – it is not a "system" which can be labelled as originating with one school of thought, one personality or cult. This is not to say that we do not owe a great deal to those individual pioneers who have given us a new way of looking at movement in this century. But it must be remembered that movement education is at least as old as the Chinese civilisation, and has been used throughout known history in rituals, ceremonies and religious observances.

In trying to describe what I think movement education is, or should really be about, the first distinction to be made is between the *content* and the *method* of presentation. Movement is something which everyone knows a great deal about either consciously or simply by being in a state of motion, vibration or activity of some kind, all the time. Just because it is such a familiar area of experience (*can* we have any experience without inner or outer movement?), and because it is transient, ever changing and ever flowing, many people find it difficult to conceive of its richness of manifestation and its all-embracing and fundamental character.

Introduction to movement study and teaching

We all know intellectually that all created things are in constant motion – not just moving about, but in ordered, patterned, rhythmical motion. Our whole world depends upon this order of moving particles: the inter-relatedness of one rhythm to another in immense subtlety and intricacy. In the physical world this is easily recognised by modern methods of observation and measuring. In the realms of thought, emotion, feeling and spiritual values, similar rhythmical patterns and forms can be discerned. The ancient wisdom, "As above, so below," recognises just this link between different levels of being. It also helps to explain why movement at one level or in one aspect of life can influence another level through this inter-relatedness.

We have now a vast accumulation of knowledge about movement. Some of it is in contemporary Western terms and easily understandable by anyone prepared to study seriously such a wealth of material. The use of a particular terminology to describe movement has frequently taken the less serious student away from the fundamentals to superficial quibbling about jargon. The wiser student, with greater knowledge, recognises that it matters little if the movement description is pictorially made ("wringing the tiger's neck," "diving for the golden needle at the bottom of the ocean," as in the T'ai Chi Ch'uan system); made almost totally through sound rhythms and patterns; caught in stone and sculptured shapes; painted on canvas; or felt directly as movement sensation in the body. One medium is more suitable than another according to circumstance and situation. Some kind of agreed terminology and notation* – a kind of shorthand – helps communication between students of movement, but experience, knowledge and recognition are primarily essential.

Just as twenty different people looking at a room might give twenty different views of it, so we find that movement is recognised from many aspects. Apart from the personal angle of

---

* There are many contemporary systems of movement notation in practical use for writing down working movements, expressive movements, ballet, dramas, etc. No doubt one of these will ultimately prove most efficient, and will be universally adopted, as is music notation.

Introduction

viewing, there are different inner attitudes of people which lead to their different awareness. There are the mechanistic viewers – those who might see the room as a floor, four walls, a ceiling, made of so many tons of bricks, concrete, tiles, etc., and held by a measurable amount of cement; others will see the room as an enclosed space, an area contained in position by the outer structure; others will see the detailed proportions, the relationships between the size of window and door and wall – the vitality of form, or its deadness; others will be aware of an atmosphere within the room – contributed by the people who live there, their belongings, decoration of the room, their thoughts and feelings; others will see the decorative details either in or out of context, and presumably there are those who will capture in this word "room" some concept of all these aspects and their relatedness one to another. So with movement: the mechanistic viewers want to test and isolate detailed measurable aspects of movement. It is quite possible to do this but it gives only a very partial view of the whole "room." The people who see movement as skilled action, at the service of an outer activity, are also dealing with one aspect of movement only. Those who teach games, gymnastics and agilities do admirable work in this field but their teaching does not provide a comprehensive movement education. This would be analogous to describing one wall as though it were the whole room. Indeed, rather than movement being relegated to a part of Physical Education, it can be seen that the traditionally based Physical Education, even when we take into account physical remedial work and the psychology of sports, could better be seen as an integral part of a whole movement education programme. Those practitioners of movement who see only dance and drama as a full movement programme are equally limited. I think it is fair to say that most teachers recognise, when they include such limited aspects in their work, that they are in fact selecting one or two personal choices from the wide range of movement activities. This may or may not lead them to introduce to their pupils the real stuff of movement – the real awakening of experience through movement and the recognition of the inter-relatedness of all things through movement – and lead them towards the formulation of inner experiences by using movement.

This is probably the crux of the whole idea of movement education. Music, poetry and painting use sound, words and colours to formulate inner experiences – so movement, the primary, most elementary, most primitive medium can be used – either for individual or group formulation. *It is not the doing of the activity which is important here, but the linking of the inner being and the outer form.* Initial expressive movements (the spontaneous activity shown in gesture and stance) are transformed into the appropriate forms of patterns and rhythms, and become not signs of emotions but symbols.

This is not a very popular educational concept today, when activity is often elevated to an educational end in itself. Most of us can fairly easily be stimulated to external activity – most of us are using this anyway as a kind of escape mechanism from developing our own inner selves. In order to formulate an inner experience it is necessary to have at our command a whole range of movement vocabulary and the capacity to use it. The teacher must therefore have some knowledge of this range, gained through personal experience as well as academic study. One's style and mixture of movement capacity is entirely personal, though the possible range is common to all human beings – and it is interesting that each species of animal has its own range, more limited than that of the human, though frequently more specialised and efficient within those limits.

As all kinds of inner capacities of man are recognisably connected with his personal movement patterns, rhythms and shapes, some development of the potential capacities is possible through the linking of inner being and outer movement. Qualities such as decisiveness, persistence, attention, ability to relate to others, leadership, etc., are seen in specific movement configurations. This is the basis of personality assessment through movement.

We are generally unaware of the patterns and rhythms of movement around us, and therefore we are frequently unable to recognise that they are all related, not only to each other but to

Introduction

ourselves. In the seemingly static as in the obviously mobile, the same kinds of laws of movement operate – at the macrocosmic level, as well as at the microcosmic and at the material as well as the non-material. This recognition leads us to a new approach in our study of man and his universe. The study of movement should lead us to become more awake and aware of ourselves, and of our relationships with others and the outer world. It is the *"principles of moving"* which must be understood and practised, not a series of specific, stereotyped movements. Movement knowledge in this sense is a tool and a material at our service. Our ability to use this material is dependent upon our individual stage of development and awareness – our individual perceptive quality and gift. As with all of us, children can respond to a level of being beyond their obvious stage of development, *i.e.*, they can respond without consciously knowing or being able to explain. This response is our own contribution and transforms the ineffable experience into a personal expression which therefore becomes a communication not only to others, but to ourselves. To accumulate facts only at their face value will not take us very far and, indeed, could well lead to stagnation and stereotypy. There is also the danger that in our constant striving for rational definitions we risk the defeat of our own aims by sacrificing meaning, *i.e.*, being rational at the expense of being reasonable. This brings us again to the idea of the symbolism of movement – that is, through experiencing movement based on universal forms,* *i.e.*, fundamental and recurrent patterns, a meaningful connection can be made between the person's inner and outer world.

How does a teacher evolve his method of presentation? Surely this is immediately connected with his personal attitude to, and understanding of, the material and medium as well as his attitude to his pupils. If he sees movement as a skill, as a performing art, or as a series of learned movement patterns, he leads his

---

* The journal *Architectural Design* (October 1965) has issued a leaflet of Universal Space Families by Keith Critchlow, showing the relatedness of crystal shapes and patterns. A movement teacher would recognise many of these as the basis of spatial harmony in movement. There are similar fundamental rhythms of audible sound in music, rhythm in movement and poetry.

pupils towards the performing of these aspects. If, however, he recognises that movement can be a medium through which a pupil can gain a broader educational experience, through which he can participate in universal rhythms, patterns and symbols – that is, become part of them, move within them, and so capture within himself as much of the essence as he is capable of receiving or mastering – then he will attempt to provide the kind of environment, stimulus and guidance which will lead to this end.

Much has already been written in other publications about the value of education through movement: the development of individual and personal capacities; the increasing social awareness; the role playing and practice in the group situation (partners, leaders, followers, and so on); the increasing poise and confidence gained through self-mastery and awareness of one's body image, etc. But a valid criticism can be made that too often in practice these values are simply not realised. Often the work is seen to be merely a bodily activity, divorced from any deeper meaning. It is quite unnecessary to have always a large space in which to hop around, although this is useful and, indeed, required on some occasions when extension and freedom in space is appropriate. But much of the real movement education takes place at other times and places than the set lesson period – times when the kinaesthetic awareness is awakened and related to external activities, to materials, to thoughts, feelings and sensations, until there is a recognition of the flow of movement in and through everything.

While admitting that some of the criticism of work seen in the schools and colleges is justified, it is also interesting to look a bit deeper at the motives behind some of the less-informed criticism. Ignorance of the aims, motives and potential of movement education can be detected in some comments; frequently there has been a condemnation without knowledge or understanding. This is not only the responsibility of the person making the criticism, but of those of us who teach, for we are sometimes too involved to see the need for adequate explanation of what we try to do, or, of course, too inadequate to make an explanation which is under-

Introduction

standable to our colleagues. Indeed, the brevity of this introduction with the need to telescope description will not be enough to clarify our position though it may call attention to the importance of communication. But there are also deeper motives for negative criticism, of which some observers of this work are not aware in themselves. *Personal self-consciousness can make people shy away from expressing themselves, but this can also lead them to "shy away" from seeing self-expression in others, even children, with concomitant resentment.* Comments intended as derogatory criticism like "it's just primitive – crude," etc., probably stem from deep personal insecurity.

I use the word "expression" with the full knowledge that different readers will interpret it in different ways. "Freedom of expression" is a catch-phrase often not defined by those using it, so that many misconceptions have arisen, not only in movement education but in educational method generally. By some, and I think happily a dwindling number, "freedom to express" is seen as an opportunity for formless, undisciplined licence. Ideas such as that children must be "uninhibited," must be allowed to "be themselves," must not have anything "imposed upon them," have led to all kinds of vague, useless self-indulgence on the part of children and students and their teachers. This would be serious enough if it were only useless and timewasting, but it can be actively negative because it impedes the growth process. Teaching requires something more than stimulating a response. It is as necessary to provide stimulating opportunity for formulation, for building a framework and a structure, as it is to allow individual contribution and invention by the pupil. For this, a "vocabulary" of movement must be available, and the presentation must incorporate within it a disciplined framework. This might be a set rhythm, set pattern, dictated form or relationship – in fact, any aspect of movement within which the pupils can make their personal contribution. Choice can only be free if it is made from experience and knowledge of what is possible, and where the person is no longer at the mercy of pure instinctual drive. As children advance in age and experience, the range of choice will

Introduction to movement study and teaching

both widen and become more subtle, *i.e.*, from a simple choice between black and white for the young child, degrees and shades of grey will gradually become available. To choose between two alternatives is the early and simple choice; between many alternatives is a later development.

Gradually, a child can be led from simple "phrases" in movement to more complex and related "sentences," from contrasting alternatives to transitional routes of changing motifs. Themes develop from simple "sentences" to comprehensive "statements," requiring formed compositions for their expression. In dramatic form, the universal or the general is reflected and constrained in the characters and the interaction between them; in the pure movement form, universal patterns, rhythms and formations are more directly experienced. For older pupils, there is a positive advantage in participating in a well-composed sequence, beyond what they themselves could have evolved. The discipline in participation is the same whether the pupils themselves create the composition, by experiment, selection and gradual formation, or whether they learn an already established form – or indeed, whether they experience a mixture of the two.

We are, of course, expecting a great deal of our movement teachers. Not only should they be able to train and lead their pupils through an experience and knowledge of the vocabulary of movement and be able to observe and help the pupils to develop, select and discern appropriate motifs and forms for their compositions, but also be to some degree creative artists themselves, able to make appropriate compositions for the varying needs of their pupils. It is therefore quite evident that a teacher attempting such a formidable task must himself have a degree of personal maturity, together with a sustained experience and real knowledge of movement. One hour a week for a year or two as a student teacher (when, after all, the student has little knowledge and experience in allied areas to relate to his movement work, and while he is still grappling with his own development and knowledge of child development) is barely a preliminary introduction. Practice in teaching will enhance his understanding and

Introduction

skill, provided that a sound basis has been acquired, and refresher courses including personal participation become the necessary nourishment for his development. These must be provided in greater profusion and of better quality than are available for the majority of interested teachers. In this sphere, some local authorities are fulfilling a great need, though in many areas nothing is offered, or so little, or of such questionable quality, that there is a kind of starvation.

Movement touches directly at a person's primary – even primitive – sensations, feelings and intuition. If we are going to dare to touch this sensitive area of being, it is well to be aware of the possible dangers as well as the possible benefits. From this point of view, those who are unaware of these deeper areas of personality, either consciously or intuitively, will do better to restrict themselves to the objective and more practical movement approach. But by so doing, they are depriving their pupils of the educative experience which perhaps can really only be given through movement. The genuinely sincere student or teacher need not be afraid of this medium, for there is an inbuilt safeguard for the sensitive and aware – that is, the safety of form, whether in rhythm or shape. These elements hold the pupil safely, while allowing him to be in touch with his primary sensations. Without this "holding" (and readers will recognise that the use of this word is related to that made by Dr Winnicott) a child could well defend himself by becoming cut off from his intuitive/sensation sides, or alternatively lose himself in a frightening, undisciplined world, reminiscent of early infancy and leading to regression. In effect, then, a movement teacher, and any good teacher, must act as mediator of the various forms of expression of his pupils, and also become the integrator by virtue of the discipline of form.

It seems that the visual and literary arts work through a different process, by translating the primary functions into a secondary medium. Movement has only the body of the person through which it works directly, while the visual arts use an outside material – colour, clay, paper, etc. – and the literary arts translate the bodily sensations into words. They therefore provide

Introduction to movement study and teaching

the security or "holding" of the pupil through the medium itself. Although no educationalist would advocate a completely free or undirected use of visual material throughout the years of schooling, perhaps less active damage can be done than through licence in the more direct art form of movement. Music – rhythm and sound, also a primary medium – has traditionally safeguarded its pupils through a stern discipline, although indeed this has sometimes worked in the opposite direction of over-rigidising and limiting, which, while avoiding licence, has thus lost the opportunities for personal development through direct formulating of inner experience through sound.

There is no substitute for the direct contact which a teacher gives his pupils. Many outer objects and situations, however, can enrich and stimulate the teaching of movement: music and sound, correctly and sensitively used, stories, mythological characters and situations, natural objects and forces, visual and poetic imagery can all contribute, and these may be immediate or through the television medium. Television could be used as an additional source of stimulus and enlarging of experience, rather than a means of teaching – and the sharing of other children's and students' work in movement could well be incorporated in this way. Both general and closed-circuit TV as well as the videotape medium could be most valuable.

Publications, photographic material and notated compositions can all help the teacher to keep in touch with others who are interested in furthering education through movement.

Movement education often exists under the doubtful umbrella of Physical Education for two main reasons: the first that some enlightened physical educationalists recognised its potential in the early days when serious movement study was first introduced in this country, and so to speak gave it "house room"; the second because this area of study is so little understood by other disciplines that there exists a kind of condescension with which we have colluded. It is likely that our insecurity has delivered us over to the existing conditions which have the effect of limiting development in our own field.

CHAPTER 1

The body is the instrument

I

THE symmetry of the body is a fundamental consideration in movement, giving a basis for the simplest form of body harmony. The opposite of this is in asymmetric movement, where one side of the body is preferred and takes the lead.

If you stand upright, evenly balanced on both feet, you can become conscious in your own body of the equality of both right and left sides. To give emphasis to the symmetry, lift your arms equally sideways and place legs evenly sideways. Feel how the body is divided down the centre by the spine, how the head is poised evenly between the two sides, giving no preference to either. A similar experience can be achieved by sitting evenly on a chair and, if you watch people in a bus or railway carriage, you will see that some habitually sit in a symmetric way, others very one-sidedly or asymmetrically.

As an exercise to experience even balance, move first to one side, stepping fully over to one leg, and stress all parts of the body on that side, reaching out from the body. Come back to centre and to an even balance. Repeat on the other side. This can be given as a simple exercise for children.

Watch someone, child or adult, walking. Very rarely will you see someone who gives an exact evenness in his or her alternate step; usually you will recognise that the step on one side is repeatedly given an accent (maybe a stress, twist, lift, drop, etc.)

Introduction to movement study and teaching

different from that on the other side. It may be difficult to distinguish which is preferred, though a difference is recognised between the two sides. Try to locate this more exactly in the body. Is it the right shoulder which comes lower than the left? Does the left hip then seem to lift higher than the right? Is there a twist round in the right hip throwing out the right foot further than the left? And so on.

Observe, if you can, the same people running, and notice what happens then. In some cases you will see a change of the individual's characteristics, while in others the same characteristics will be repeated, perhaps emphasised or lessened. Walking or running is essentially an alternation of asymmetric movement.

Try for yourself standing with the weight shifted over to one side, then the other side, then again evenly. You might recognise that one or other position feels more familiar to you and that you habitually choose one or other stance. This can contribute to the familiar body position which your friends would recognise from some distance.

Watch people sitting – in chairs, on the floor, in trains – and notice the differences from this point of view. Some lean or bend to one side, some sit evenly balanced. Even those who are carrying their weight evenly often give preference to one side with the head leaning or bending over.

In everyday activity and action, it is most common to see the body used in an asymmetric way. We grasp, write, throw and pick up usually with one hand (most commonly the right, but some people prefer the left). This is easy to observe and recognise, because the focus is on the actual handling of material. What is also interesting to see is what the rest of the body does at this time: does it make an active balance, or does it remain passive? Where does the head go? Leaning over or away from the active hand? Or does it maintain an impartial uprightness? This brings to our notice the aspect of balance once more, but this time through two contrasting positions of different body parts; that is, asymmetric balance (as opposed to symmetric balance).

The body is the instrument

USING THIS EXPERIENCE TO STIMULATE CREATIVE MOVEMENT

No dance or dramatic action sequence is limited to any one aspect of movement; such an extreme limitation leads only as far as exercise. Dance or drama by its nature will always unify the varying aspects of movement: the rhythm, shape and bodily agility or awareness. It is possible, however, to select one aspect of movement which can be given preference and stress; that is,

Fig. 1 Elevation

one dance will be more rhythmical, or another more concerned with shape, or another with body positions.

The particular theme of this chapter – symmetry and asymmetry – can be used in movement exercise and for stimulus in dance or drama.

Exploratory approach

This is most suitable for young children or adult beginners. Great caution should be used in this method of presentation to young people, twelve to fifteen or sixteen years of age. With some groups it may be possible, but it is not generally recommended.

Examples of movement ideas used as a challenge for the class to respond freely are as follows:

(*a*) Balance weight evenly on both feet, then on one foot and then on the other.

(*b*) Choose a new place in the room and when you have arrived there stop quite still balanced on one leg. (This can at first be controlled by the teacher by, for instance, sound accompaniment but soon the children should decide for themselves when to go and when to arrive.) The teacher's responsibility is to present this in a play-way, so that the children enjoy the sensation of these actions, and work over a period on such bodily play. Extension of the idea comes (as we observed earlier) in balancing on other parts of the body (as in sitting evenly or over on one side), but for children this is even more fundamental and near to their experience – on knees, hands, elbows, shoulders, etc.

(*c*) Travelling, making one side of the body more important or both equal, using character types walking, or more dance-like movements which result in hopping and jumping or turning (*see* Fig. 1).

The aim should not be to limit the work to isolated experiences, but ultimately to link them into a dance-like sequence which can be simple or more complicated according to the needs of the class.

Dance exercise approach

With older children and adults, it is helpful and necessary to present definite dance exercises. Even within the exploratory stage, it is often an advantage to intersperse specific movement exercises and not leave all the choice and decision to the individual. By so doing, a certain balance of the freedom comes through a unison discipline, and extends the range of movement beyond the limitation of each person's own choice.

The body is the instrument

Each teacher can work out his or her own dance exercises. Such definite exercises can be presented with exact detail of step, jump, turn, etc., or more generally, *e.g.*, right-side moves, left-side moves, both.

II

If you stretch out in front of you as though reaching for something a long way away, or for an object almost out of reach, and grasp the object and bring it close to you, almost certainly you will have used your hand for this, although it was not stipulated. You will also have extended your fingers out in reaching, if only a little way, and brought them together when grasping the object. You will have bent up your arm, or curled it round, in bringing the object closer to your body. Repeat this action several times, concentrating now on the extending of the arms and hands on the outward stretch and the folding in of the parts of the arms and hands as they approach the body.

Stand up and step on to a stool or stairs and, before the weight is taken up, notice the bending of the leg as it folds nearer towards the body centre. As the weight is transferred upwards, the leg extends to normal. Make several such bendings and stretchings of the leg, bending upwards nearer the body, and stretching out down to the floor. Stand evenly and bend the knees and ankles, gradually sinking down until the extreme folding together comes in kneeling down.

Similarly, in the spine, bending and stretching is experienced in our frequent changes of position, *e.g.*, bending down to pick up something or reaching up to a high shelf.

The coming closer together of two parts of the body gives a narrowness (or nearness) and contrasts with extension (or farness) of the one part from another.

Introduction to movement study and teaching

Observe in everyday life that, in walking, the legs have a greater or lesser degree of bending and stretching. In some cases it will be observed that the knees are never really stretched, or one knee is kept more bent, giving a definite character to the walk. In running, the legs probably become more bent and certainly need more elasticity and resilience in extending and contracting.

In carrying, picking up and holding, the arms and hands are used. Observe how differently the objects can be grasped: with the whole hand, and fingertips, with both hands, with thumb and finger or even with the whole arm for very large objects. This can be performed either symmetrically or asymmetrically.

The relationship between different parts of the body becomes significant; for example, in a dramatic situation, where the policeman grasps the shoulder of the thief (hand grips shoulder), or in shaking hands (hand grips hand), or expressively gripping the hands together in horror (own hands grip).

USING THIS EXPERIENCE TO STIMULATE CREATIVE MOVEMENT

Exploratory approach

The movement experience of curling up the body (either slightly or very tightly gripped) and stretching it out can go beyond the physical achievement of these actions. The inner focus and concentration experienced in a curled position is a contrast with the outward focusing experienced in extending away from the centre of the body. We can use such ideas as covering oneself and opening out two parts of the body – say, an arm and opposite leg – making them fly out away from each other, and creep together, or a game involving various parts touching or gripping, getting stuck together, one part chasing another, and so on. Here clapping and clicking sounds can be used.

Example of an asymmetric dance exercise

The sequence can be performed on the spot with arms only, or with stepping or jumping, or introducing variations, with perhaps

The body is the instrument

a turn on the gathering or the scattering movement. Try out these various combinations.

> Starting position   wide, with extra stress on the right side
> 1st movement   right side gathers, left side makes natural closing movement in support
> 2nd movement   right side opens wide, left side opens also in support, but less actively

The movement is repeated on the same side.

In the early stages (primary), it is important that the child becomes confident and free in a "play" form; self-invented sequences and actions gradually develop into longer, composed dance forms, which need an awareness of selection and discrimination. Older primary children and young secondary pupils who have this background experience can quickly develop their work into composed dances and dance dramas. This step between movement play and dancing as an artistic activity shows in the gradual acquisition of definite dances which can be repeated. At this level, there is a place for dances taught by the teacher, in order to extend the children's experience beyond their own invention. There is no definite age at which this happens; older primary children enjoy whole dance forms and can well achieve a high degree of absorption and experience from participating in appropriate compositions.

CHAPTER 2

The movements of the body have different accents and stress

RECOGNISE AND OBSERVE

WE learn quickly to recognise footsteps of people even before they come into view: outside a door, going upstairs, pacing up and down. This recognition is made because of the very individual characteristics of our walk which result in the production of a sequence of sounds (that is, into audible movement). In one, we notice the continuous slurring of the feet giving a smooth preliminary sound before the step placement; in another, the definite placement of a purposeful heel regularly and evenly, like a military step; in another, a sharp click! click! quick and precise; another will have a methodical and slow placement; another, an irregular, longer and shorter interval between the sounds; another an evenness of length, but a decided stress on one step, and less on the other. Such a repetitive movement of the body, as in stepping, gives us an opportunity to study just how and where an accent is placed in relation to the less stressed part of the movement.

Become aware of the sound patterns which are made by different people when they walk, and write these down. Also try to write down your own pattern of walking. Then recognise the natural differences between a young child's eager walk and the steady "going along" of an adult. As people become more automatic in their walking, it is usual that a regularity arises but with children an irregular accent will frequently intervene: a

The movements of the body

sudden break into a few running steps, a jump in the air, slowing down in reluctance, and seemingly irrelevant variations which reflect changing inner moods and attitudes. A child learning to walk is still striving towards the achievement of balance and regular alternation of steps and the automatisation grows slowly, so that a most irregular sound pattern results.

The contact of the foot on the floor in walking and running gives a chance to "observe" movement through hearing sounds but this is not possible in all movements of the body. There are, nevertheless, similar stresses and accents in movements which make no sound : in twisting round to look at something behind, in describing the shape of something with the hands, in reaching out to pick up something, in beckoning someone to come, in pointing to a place, etc. In a spoken sentence it makes a difference which word is stressed (and many advertisements play on this idea). In the written word we underline the stressed word, so it means something different if I say :

"*I* shall come" (as distinct from someone else).
"I *shall* come" (asserting my intention).
"I shall *come*" (emphasising my future action).

In the same way, a "movement sentence" means something quite different if it starts impulsively and dies away, or if the accent is at the middle of the phrase, or if the phrase is built up to an impactive and definite movement at the end of the phrase. You will see that such an idea has taken us away from the more easily observed movement of walking, which is repetitive and automatised.

Try to observe where the accent appears in a movement phrase, in a gesture, or in an action of any kind. It may be that there is no discernible accent and the movement retains an evenness and equal stress throughout (in an exaggerated form, perhaps like a sleepwalker who moves "in a dream"), but usually certain emphasised and accentuated parts of movement can be distinguished, and of course there is frequently more than one accent

Introduction to movement study and teaching

in a movement phrase. Let us look at what kind of accent this can be. On the one hand, there may be distinct variations in the urgency or leisureliness of a movement. On the other hand, there can be a difference of force and drive, and frequently these two things are combined. An impulsive person usually bursts out with an idea, a gesture, or an action, with explosive suddenness together with energy and drive (whether this drive is always carried through to the completion of the action is another point). It may be that a different kind of impulsive person has only these sudden flashes of ideas without the drive to do anything with them, and this would be revealed in movement phrases where sudden beginnings can be noticed, followed by a falling off or dying away, so that no real ending is made. Contrasting with this fading away movement, there can be discerned those actions which build up to a climax, getting either more urgent or stronger or both, and finishing with an accent. The different inner meanings revealed through such movements can be experienced. For instance, make a gesture beckoning someone to come to you in both ways, and be aware of the different implication in these two gestures; one is much more impelling than the other. Or make a simple action of placing a book on a table, first with an impactive thrusting down, then with an impulsive beginning and quiet placement.

The *phrase* is as important in movement as the sentence or phrase in speech or writing. Unphrased movement is vague and meaningless and leads to meandering muddle. The meaning of a movement phrase can be discerned by the precision of the beginning, the clarity of the action, and the clear ending. The beginning is usually a position which is related to the forthcoming action: a bodily and mental preparation. The ending arises out of the previous action and is a natural conclusion of it.

For instance, a movement whose action is *travelling* from one place to another might stress a high, towering position, ready to swoop to a new place in the room. The ending could be close to the floor, touching the floor with hands as well as feet.

An action of *turning* might have as a preparation a closing of

The movements of the body

the body, leaning to one side, ready to open out and turn.

An action of *closing* might have an open, extended position, ready to close.

An action of *elevation* might have a downward, backward, leaning position, ready to exert energy to push off the ground.

Travelling

This means the transferring of the body from one place in the room to another. This is normally performed by the feet and legs carrying the weight of the body in walking or running, but can also be performed by other parts of the body taking the weight, *e.g.*, in rolling or more agile activities like walking on the hands, seat, etc. Young people, and children particularly, seem to enjoy this more primitive rolling and other agile activity, while adults and older people do not.

Turning

This means facing a new direction, making a quarter, half, three-quarters, whole turn or even more. During the turn, the body may be held in a stable, upright, balanced position, or it may be moving off the stable upright in more mobile, diagonal positions. In the latter case there will be continuous readjustment of the body poise. The body may make an opening movement during the turn, or a closing movement during the turn, or may retain a constant position. The opening or closing of the body in exaggerated extension may in fact lead to the turning movements.

Opening and closing of the body

The body is so constructed that movements of closing, grasping and bending contrast with movements of opening, releasing and stretching. When the whole body participates, it becomes crouched and rounded in closing, extended and spread out in opening. It is also possible to make these actions with only part of the body, *e.g.*, the legs extending or opening wide, the arms, shoulders and upper body closing and narrowing. If one side of the body is mainly stressed, an asymmetric movement and position results which leads naturally to further movement, whereas symmetry tends to lead to a position of arrival.

Introduction to movement study and teaching

Jumping

This means the elevation of the whole body or parts of the body into the air.

Before any of the actions can be performed, it is necessary for the teacher to prepare the class by suggesting an appropriate starting situation. This will be a physical position, together with the appropriate inner attitude. For instance, in jumping there will tend to be a downward preparation; in turning, a sideways preparation, and so on. The ending of the phrase of movement during which the action takes place must be concerned with an adequate recovery, and, if the action is repeated, there will be a recovery after each phrase. Frequently these recoveries merge with a new preparation for action in the subsequent phrase.

SOME EXAMPLES OF SIMPLE ACTION SEQUENCES
IN PHRASES

Travelling

Stepping with a pause between each phrase:

(*a*) Step, step, step, pause with feet together.
(*b*) Run, run, run, run, run, pause.
(*c*) Rolling smoothly on to feet.

All phrases can be repeated to form longer sentences of movement. It is necessary to know clearly where the phrase starts, what action takes place and where the phrase ends.

Turning

(*a*) Whirling like a top, dying down and pause.
(*b*) Facing front, facing side wall, facing back wall, facing other side wall and front again (with or without a pause in each new direction).

Opening and closing

(*a*) A gradual unfolding like a breath to a held position, fully extended; then pause. A following phrase could be shrinking

The movements of the body

back in one action, like an exhalation of breath.

(b) Simple hand actions of curling in and spreading, using the fingers in sequence and with a clear flow of action.

Jumping

Rhythmical springing actions, with buoyancy and resilience:

up	up	up
resilient	resilient	down to
bounce	bounce	touch ground

COMBINATIONS OF ACTIONS IN PHRASES

Each action can be performed alone as in the above examples, or in combination with one another, which results in more natural action.

Combinations of two actions

Jumping and opening or closing during the jump, *e.g.*, jumping as in the example above on the spot, opening wide in the air, and closing when coming down from the jump.

Jumping and turning during the jump, *e.g.*, springing into the air and landing facing a new direction.

Jumping and travelling during the jump, *i.e.*, jumping away from the spot.

Turning with opening or closing during the turn.

Turning with travelling from one place to another.

Travelling with a jump – either leaping repetitively, or varying the time spent in each part of the action.

Travelling with a turn during the travelling.

Travelling with opening or closing the body.

Opening or closing with a jump.

Opening or closing with a turn.

Opening or closing travelling through the room.

Combinations of three actions

Combinations of three actions can be stressed with the main action and two subsidiary actions:

Jumping
>With turning and travelling
>With turning and opening or closing
>With travelling and opening or closing

Turning
>With jumping and travelling
>With jumping and opening or closing
>With travelling and opening or closing

Travelling
>With jumping and opening or closing
>With jumping and turning
>With turning and opening or closing

Opening or closing
>With jumping and travelling
>With jumping and turning
>With turning and travelling

This will be seen as a simple permutation of actions.

All four actions may be combined with any one action stressed. For instance, turning with jumping, travelling and opening and closing or jumping with turning, travelling and opening and closing, etc. The presentation of these movement sequences can only be through movement phrases. If only one action is used, appropriate preparations have been suggested. In combined actions, combined preparations are necessary. It cannot be too frequently repeated that movement phrases are essential. A movement phrase consists of preparation, the action and its recovery. There may, of course, be many phrases linked together in repetition or in developing sequences.

USING THIS EXPERIENCE TO STIMULATE CREATIVE MOVEMENT: AN EXPLORATORY APPROACH

The whole body can travel to a new place, starting calmly and smoothly, gradually increasing in speed, urgency and power, until

The movements of the body

it arrives with a jump. This may be taken freely or with a definite length of phrase as a unison movement. Contrast this with an explosive beginning which continues, gradually fading away (the kind of movement in sound which a gong gives when played with a single stroke). Such a link between movement accents and sounds is a valuable one to pursue (*see* Chapter 9 on the use of percussion as a stimulus for movement) but the group should not become dependent entirely upon an outside sound, and sometimes each person can accompany himself with voice or instrument in relation to and following his own movement pattern. A series of shorter phrases built into a "sentence" or a repetitive accent can be made. The awareness of the accents should be developed in all parts of the body as an inner bodily sensation which has nothing to do with metrical beat or counting time. The sensitive accompanying by voice sounds of the movement of other people awakens and encourages the observation and enlarges an individual's own experiences.

Increasingly difficult variations can be made by an extension of the phrase to include more than one "statement."

CHAPTER 3

Activity and recovery

WE saw in the last chapter how phrases of movement can reveal quite different tendencies of a person's intention, according to where an accent or stress is made in the phrase. We now consider why these accents occur and why some movements are unstressed, or less stressed than others.

In a general sense, accent (or activity or effort) is always a striving to do something, "to make an effort," to get a job done. This implies action, whether it appears as a mental action, like a thought or idea, or whether it is a more easily discernible body action, like standing up, writing a letter and so on. Nature insists that, if we make an effort, we ultimately need a recovery from that effort, just as in nature night follows day, the seasons come in order, and the calm comes after the storm. So the human body recovers regularly, in sleeping daily, by breaks from working and, perhaps less regularly, in recreative activities. But even in our short-term actions or efforts we demand and need a recovery. Watch a child writing for some considerable period and you will see his wriggling body, stretching of the arms, screwing up of the face and, if allowed, usually he will stand up or walk and jump about. This recovery takes the form of a new action and it is likely to be quite vigorous as a compensation for the restrictive and small movements he needed in writing. So we see that a vigorous action or effort may also be a recovery. What is usually termed "relaxation," that is, a physical releasing of tension (and thereby a mental release also), is one valuable form of recovery. This cannot be used exclusively (no one wants only to sleep when

Activity and recovery

not working) and recreation is our means of actively building up our inner resources after working. As an example, we will look at a working action, lifting heavy objects from one place to another. In between each action the workman gets his recovery by releasing his body tension before picking up the next object.

In repetitive actions which occur in our present factory systems, one of the main difficulties for a person, say on the conveyor belt, is to adapt his effort to the regular and repetitive action necessary to keep up with the work. Those who manage this best have probably an innate capacity for metrical action, coupled with a skilful use of regular compensatory movements. These compensatory movements are not necessarily a relaxation and "giving up" in between each action. In this way the alternations of action and recovery create a certain pattern in time and energy, where compensation is achieved without interruption. One who never compensates for his actions will not be able to continue over a long period without strain, though of course this is not the only cause of mental strain in a job.

Try to observe some repetitive actions and notice how the efficiency is greater, as is also the feeling of well-being, when action and recovery flow easily together.

Another aspect of efficient action is that adequate preparation is always needed. This may take the form of light, unstressed movements preceding a vigorous punch or it might be a strong gathering of inner tension before a fine and sensitive handling of delicate objects. In repetitive action, the recovery and preparation may fuse together. A wrong preparation can easily ruin the efficiency of the action. For instance, there is a limit to endurance if a continuously strong movement – a punch, a pressure, a squeezing and so on – is maintained without a compensation of relaxation or lightness, and the strength efficiency decreases. Similarly, a fine touch or light action cannot be continuously sustained without becoming heavy unless there is a recovery and a new preparation.

Practise this for yourself. Make a continuous gliding or smoothing movement without interruption, and feel how the movement

Introduction to movement study and teaching

loses its lightness after a while. Then make the same movements in a series of phrases of preparation, glide and release. Then the fine touch can be recaptured.

Now make a different movement: a strong punching action. Try to do this over and over again, keeping in a constant state of tension and grip. Not only is this exhausting, but it becomes ineffective and then either cramp or weakness. Try instead a series of punching actions: preparation (by a lighter gathering movement), punch, punch, punch and relax. This is much less tiring and could be repeatedly maintained over a much longer period.

Become aware in your own body of natural rhythmical alternations: the heartbeat (a regular time-keeper which varies according to our condition, excitement, tiredness, etc., but cannot be consciously controlled), and the breathing in and out (which can be somewhat controlled and therefore utilised as a way of influencing our body-mind mechanics).

VARIATIONS OF PHRASING AND RHYTHM

Natural body movement is always in phrases or sentences of movement. The observable differences of movement happenings can be discerned in two distinct ways: the measurable and mechanical aspects, and the qualitative or personal aspects. In every phrase, therefore, attention can be given to the rhythmical build-up from both points of view.

The time aspect of rhythm and phrasing

(*a*) A regular or irregular beat, and the division into long and short values as well as the overall speed and acceleration or deceleration.

(*b*) The attitude of the moving person towards the quality of time, at the one extreme moving with urgency and suddenness and, at the other extreme, moving with sustainment and in a leisurely manner. It will be recognised that these two contrasting attitudes have a difference in mood and inner

Activity and recovery

participation. Inner participation can be provoked by the movement itself; for example, the stimulus of lively, gay movement provokes a lively inner attitude. Alternatively, the provocation of the group towards a particular inner mood through words or an imaginative idea can provoke the kind of movement required. For instance, the idea of stepping on hot bricks or chasing one's feet provokes a definite action response with an emotional content. The tone of voice can give a definite mood content to a simple action of, say, spreading out, and music can provoke an inner mood; for instance, a solemn ritual in a simple stepping action or the dying away of sound which stimulates a weakening, settling, sinking relaxation.

Using only the ideas with which we have dealt so far, a simple phrase of movement could be invented. This example is only one of many which are possible.

The starting position is close, near the body. The first movement is an asymmetric opening out with a turn. There is a pause and a holding of the position in a symmetric balance, wide and spread out. The upper part of the body is stressed. The next movement is an advancing to meet a partner or group and at the same time the body narrows symmetrically. Here the main action is in the legs and feet in advancing, supported by the arms in reaching forward. The focus is on the partner. The movement develops by the taking of hands, the spinning together, the breaking away from each other, and the inward closing towards oneself again.

This is a description from two points of view:

Action. Opening out followed by travelling, followed by turning, followed by closing. Simultaneous movement occurs, and a joining of hands with a partner.

Symmetry. The body is used at first asymmetrically, then symmetrically; the upper part of the body is leading some parts of the sequence, the legs leading other parts.

This sequence can be varied or developed by recognising the

Introduction to movement study and teaching

particular use of the time quantity and quality which affects the phrasing. For instance:

Phrase 1 might be slowly opening, increasing speed with a poised pause at the end.
Phrase 2, a quick advancing development of steps to meet the partner. (This can be either regular or irregular in timing.)
Phrase 3, a quick whirling and breakaway into decreasing speed and slowly returning to the closed starting position.

All these aspects of time are from a quantitative point of view: the measurable aspect. It is also possible to develop the sequence from the "quality of mood" aspect of time and, in this case, we should see the following:

Phrase 1, a calm, tentative, hesitant, leisurely opening, as though there is infinite time and a gradual loss of hesitancy, finishing wide in the pause.
Phrase 2, performed with lively, urgent, repetitive steps (as though anxious to meet the partner).
Phrase 3, with explosive, exuberant whirling, and a sudden breakaway and a gradual turn to finish in a calm, leisurely closing into self.

Summary of above sequence

	Phrase 1	*Phrase* 2	*Phrase* 3
Action	opening out	travelling	turning and closing
Measurable time aspects	slow, with increasing speed	quick	quick, decreasing to slow
Quality and mood of time	starting tentative, hesitant, becoming more lively before the end	lively, urgent, sudden	explosive, whirling, exuberant, changing gradually after the break into smooth, calm leisureliness

Activity and recovery

Note that the words are quite different according to the aspects of movement required. The words that the teacher or leader uses will provoke particular and different responses from the class and it is important to consider them in planning the lesson.

It will be noticed that, if the measurable aspects only are stressed, the movement is mechanical and that, when the qualities of liveliness and calmness (that is, the suddenness and sustainment) are used, they give meaning to the movement in a more expressive and dance-like way.

The accent aspect of rhythm and phrasing

The accent or stress within the movement can be the measurable degree of force ranging from weakness to forcefulness, or the attitude of lightness or sensitivity or its contrast of firmness and strength.

The flow aspect of rhythm and phrasing

The flow of the movement can be the continuity and smoothness, as against the jerkiness and interrupted flow (*i.e.*, the measurable aspects), or the inner attitude of restraint and withholding (bound flow) and its contrast of freedom and ease (free flow), *i.e.*, the quality of mood aspect.

The spatial aspect of rhythm and phrasing

This can be the straightness or twistedness of the angles (the measurable aspect of space), or the attitude of flexibility contrasted with directness in focus and body movements (the quality aspect of space).

Let us return to our example of the simple sequence of movement in three phrases and develop it further:

> Phrase 1, which is opening slowly with sustainment and finishing with a pause. The interest here could be increased by bringing in a new quality of movement, that is, light and gentle at the beginning, changing gradually into a firm held position (*i.e.*, the aspect of stress or accent is also considered). The phrase could start with this lightness in a restrained manner, becoming freer as the movement opens wider, and then could

Introduction to movement study and teaching

be held with a firm binding of the flow of movement during the pause (*i.e.*, the flow aspect). It could be flexible, becoming much more directed as the phrase develops (*i.e.*, the space aspect). All these amplifications together build the complete phrase.

Phrase 2. The quick, lively travelling towards the partner could be with light stepping, with a free, easy flow and a direct focus; *i.e.*, the stress is light, the flow is free, the focus is direct.

Phrase 3 (which has a transition of the touch and grip with strength) could be whirling with free flow, with strength, and with directness. The breakaway could be sudden, freer becoming bound, stronger becoming gentle and light, and quicker becoming slower. A degree of flexibility could also be introduced in the last, settling into the closed position.

The whole sequence above is summarised in the table on page 23.

Such analysis is useful to the teacher for the composition of phrases or sequences. Not every aspect which is mentioned can possibly or desirably be equally stressed with every other, and certainly in the presentation to the class only one idea should be highlighted at a time. Of course, any one of the three phrases could be taken repeatedly with a transition in between. For instance, in Phrase 1, there could be, after the first opening, a movement back to closing, with a new opening again, a sinking back, and a third opening until finally there is the full enjoyment of the wide symmetric position. Phrase 2 could be elongated by the meeting of one partner, and a turning away and meeting of a new partner, before the whirling. Phrase 3 has a natural transition from the action to the beginning of the sequence again.

The example above is only one possible composition, and one possible sequence of variations given the above initial actions. The initial opening could have been strong and vital, the travelling hesitant and jerky, the turning together smooth and resilient, and many other variations could be evolved.

When the teacher is clear about the composition, the phrasing

Activity and recovery

Summary of sequence on page 21

	Phrase 1	Phrase 2	Phrase 3(a)	Phrase 3(b)
Action	opening (with travelling)	travelling forward	turning	breakaway and closing
Body	asymmetric; upper part of body stressed	symmetric; legs leading; arms outstretched	gripping partner	asymmetric
Phrase and rhythm				
Time: quantity	slow < quick (pause)	quick	quick	quick < slow
quality	calm < lively	lively	lively	lively < sustained
Stress: quantity	light < forceful	light	light	forceful < light
quality	sensitive < firm or gentle	sensitive < strong grip	sensitive	firm < gentle
Flow: quantity	smooth < held	smooth	smooth	jerk < smooth
quality	free < bound	free, easy	free	free < bound
Space: quantity	twisted < straight	straight	straight	straight < twisted
quality	flexible < direct	direct	direct	direct < flexible
Relationship with others	alone, focusing at the end towards a partner or group across the space	towards the partner gripping hands	with partner	alone
Pathway and pattern	starting near the body, finishing wide; rising from deep to high level, with spiral pathway	forward extension at medium level	medium level (or this could vary)	sinking in spiral to floor

23

Introduction to movement study and teaching

will naturally follow. Any music which an accompanist might play will depend entirely upon the variations and upon the timing stimulated by the teacher. Naturally, if there is a freedom of choice in timing for the members of the group, no unison movement will result and music for the group will not be possible.

USING THIS EXPERIENCE TO STIMULATE MOVEMENT: AN EXPLORATORY APPROACH

It should be clear from the movement sequences suggested above that in stimulating activity where the *quality* of the action is mainly important a correct stimulus is necessary. In a free way, children can enjoy repeating large body actions: punching, chopping, sawing in continuous sequences. Left to themselves, most children will develop their own natural sequences of preparation, action and recovery. This comes from a spontaneous harmonising of movement which is innate in man. In mastering other people's rhythms it may be helpful to work in unison with a partner or a larger group and, in this case, a common rhythm will develop. The teacher must decide at what stage this unison work can be included. Older people starting the practice of movement often find this unison working a greater stimulus at the beginning than developing an individual rhythm.

When it is necessary to give an outer stimulus to the movement sequences, two main points should be kept in mind:

(*a*) The starting situation from which the preparation and action can arise. Given the opportunity, such as the order "Go into a starting place from which you can begin your chopping (hitting, smoothing, etc.)," most children discover naturally the best situation, and it is valuable for the moving person to be led to discover this himself.

(*b*) The need for appropriate phrasing of the order ("preparation and go," "preparation, go and release," etc.) according to the desired sequence. The preparation may be, for instance, only a momentary and small movement like a gathering and an intake of breath before a repeated vigorous

Activity and recovery

punching, or it may take the form of a long swinging curve taking much longer than the actual action, like the preparation of a tennis serve. Teachers should be aware that the rhythmical sequences of young children are usually speedier than those of adults, and it is well to observe the timing of spontaneous rhythmical sequences of the children before trying to give one to them which might be too adult. All kinds of working actions can be used to stimulate the exploration of different kinds of activity, not only strong and vigorous ones but the more sensitive light ones. The practice of such action sequences, with adequate compensatory movements, is an invigorating experience and helps to develop the bodily feeling and mastery of different qualities and ways of moving, just as in painting, when different colours and textures are selected.

Recovery through a natural rebound or resilience is also part of this experience. The resiliency of a movement has a kind of springing action, for instance a repeated rebound may be seen in some walking actions of people with resilient steps.

Longer phrases and combinations of more varied actions make a greater challenge to the child, *e.g.*, light running steps (preparation), jump (action), landing (recovery), new movement of three light, sudden steps retreating.

CHAPTER 4

The body moves into different zones of space

I

IF you bend knees, ankles and hips until finally kneeling on the ground, you become aware that your body makes a gradually releasing resistance to the pull of gravity, and that the usual upright position is one which overcomes and conquers the pull down towards the ground. Contrast this pull away from gravity by looking up, lifting higher the whole body, until you feel you could fly off the ground.

Stand in a normal everyday position – then droop a bit, focus downwards, and experience the different inner concentration from that which arises with a stance where you focus upwards. This can also happen in sitting and walking.

Now observe people sitting, walking and standing. They reveal a great deal of their momentary mood or habitual outlook in their depressed drooping and sagging of the body, giving in to gravity, or their buoyant and lively upward spring. A very young child is happier on or near the floor, with many parts of the body supporting him – hands and knees, seat and legs, etc. – and only gradually learns to like and to repeat a more upright posture. Jumping off the ground – the greatest resistance to gravity of which we are capable – is a later pleasure for children and one which they acquire gradually in their development.

Observe also any counter-tendencies in the body towards this upward or downward focus; perhaps one side is more frequently

The body moves into different zones of space

lifted or sinking down. Perhaps the body is lifted, but the eyes look down.

In our practical everyday life of handling material, it is usually the weight of the material handled which dictates this pull or resistance towards or away from gravity in our movement: a heavy bag will weigh down the body on the carrying side, or the back, wherever it is placed. It is difficult to have any feeling of elevation in the body when handling weighty material. But if you watch someone continuously doing a heavy job, you will often see him stretch his body, not only straightening out cramped muscles, but also enjoying the sensation of lifting away from this earth-bound job, and usually this will be accompanied by a deep breath which helps the airy, rising feeling.

It is not only into the upper and lower regions of space that our body moves, but into other areas around us. If you notice a whole group of people listening to a lecture or story, you will see those who press forward eagerly, and those who retreat backwards in their whole body attitude. Some poke their heads forward as they walk, others lean the whole body, as though anxious to arrive a second earlier. Others have a tendency towards a backward leaning, as though reluctant to arrive. Similarly there will be in some people an inclination towards the area on the right side of the body or the left. Observe these varied inclinations of the body in space, together with any counter-indications in different parts of the body. Frequently there is an alternating inclination between right and left or backward and forward, almost a doubting which to choose.

VARIATIONS IN PATHWAYS AND PATTERN

1. The body can move towards different directions. In a simple form this can be considered as:
 (*a*) upwards and downwards,
 (*b*) sideways (open) and sideways (across the body),
 (*c*) forwards and backwards.

These directions are always in relation to the body, so that if,

Introduction to movement study and teaching

for instance, a turn is made, the "front" turns to a new place in the room, *i.e.*, the front of the body always remains front.

For more experienced groups, it is good to turn the class to face other directions in the room to establish this orientation in relation to the body rather than to use always the room walls and corners for help in establishing direction.

Contrasting with these dimensional directions which lead to stable, balanced movement positions, account can be taken of diagonal direction, *i.e.*, diagonal movements have a pull of three dimensions together:

> high, right, forward moving to deep, left, backwards
> high, right, backwards moving to deep, left, forward
> high, left, backwards moving to deep, right, forward
> high, left, forward moving to deep, right, backwards

It is helpful to think of the body moving in a sphere, like a ball inside which we move. (See Laban's book, *Modern Educational Dance,* for further details of space harmony and relationships.) The ball or sphere turns, jumps, travels, shrinks and expands with us. The specific directions mentioned above are observable positions or places in this sphere, and the awareness of such clear placements helps to clarify the movement. There are, of course, many other directions which can be fixed in space, and notably the twelve directional stresses:

high right	high left	deep left	deep right
right back	right forward	left forward	left back
backward deep	forward deep	forward high	backward high

Briefly, the clarity of movement resulting from an awareness of specific directions within the movement shape can help:

(a) In observing position, *e.g.*, the body reaching high, or the body in a balanced poise with right arm sideways forward, the left arm left, the left leg backward deep and the head to high right backward.

The body moves into different zones of space

(*b*) In observing movement, *e.g.*, with a circular swinging action of the upper part of the body in a closing movement, beginning backward high, spreading and passing sideways open, forward, ending in deep sideways, with the body closed and kneeling on the ground. This could lead to the action of turning with or without a jump and, if a transition is made from deep sideways to backward high, there could be a repetitive travelling turning jump.

2. The directions used in any particular movement phrase may be:

(*a*) From the body centre, outwards or from outside towards the body centre.

(*b*) Surrounding and enclosing the body, never touching the centre. (*See* further notes in part II of this chapter.)

3. The nearness of the movement to the body or its wide spreading extension gives a different expression to the same movement. The easiest and most everyday movement occurs within the easy reach of the body, neither very close nor very extended. In composing sequences, these variations will give greater meaning and encourage whole body/mind participation.

4. The different levels of movement can be distinguished as:

high level
medium level
deep level.

The experience of each level with its characteristic movement should be brought to a group. At first, it is a good idea to check the various sequences presented during a lesson, to see whether there is not any undue stress on any one level or an exclusion of one (perhaps due to the teacher's own movement make-up). Sequences can be composed which remain solely or mainly at one level, or they can be composed deliberately to involve a continuous change of level.

5. Floor patterns arise from the kind of movement action chosen, though it is possible to have some preconceived arrangement along which the movement travels. It is important that the

Introduction to movement study and teaching

movement shape and form and the air pattern relate to the floor pattern, and a good way of composition seems to be to let the movement dictate the floor pattern.

USING THIS EXPERIENCE TO STIMULATE CREATIVE MOVEMENT

Examples of the exploratory approach

(a) Crouch down on the ground and look into the whole area of space above your head. Begin to grow into this space above, reaching high out, first with one side (most easily the hand) and the rest of the body following. Taken freely this exploration of the space above leads to flying upwards freely in the room, jumping to get higher or, as a smaller extension, only a striving

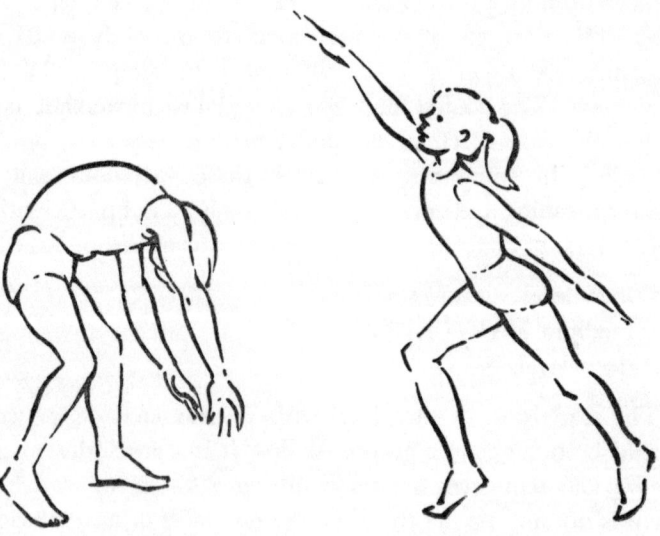

Fig. 2 (*left*) Bowing down Fig. 3 (*right*) Moving forward and high

towards this elevation. Infinite variation comes with the introduction of different approaches – eagerly, reluctantly, cautiously, explosively, passively, etc. – as well as leading the movement with different parts of the body, *e.g.*, the back, chin, knee, hip,

The body moves into different zones of space

and not only fingertips.

(*b*) Poising high, looking down, as from a mountain top, to the space below, climb down, shoot, dive, sink or relax down into this area, touching the ground with a chosen part of the body. Emphasise this deepness by travelling across the floor always in contact with it, *i.e.*, rolling, crawling, etc.

(*c*) Alternate between the rising and sinking movement, on the spot, travelling, sometimes staying high or low for a time in between, sometimes pausing in one position before going on. This can be taken quite freely, each person choosing his or her own way, or can be organised and regulated as a unison movement, still leaving variation of direction of movement.

(*d*) Contrast simple stepping down, with high toe stepping or jumping. This helps to develop the experience of the different areas. Characterising can be a natural development, *e.g.*, of the drooping and dejected tramp or the lively and buoyant excitement of a child (*see* Figs. 2 and 3).

(*e*) Similar exploration play between side to side and forward and backward movements can be made.

(*f*) Dramatic movement play between partners, one above the other, the subjugated one responding by edging away, bowing down in front, etc. (*i.e.*, question and answer in movement).

Dance exercise approach

For an exact dance training try out various combinations, also with the movements of the previous lessons, *e.g.*

Starting position	high
1st movement	to forward medium (or everyday) level
2nd movement	continue the sinking down to deep near the floor
3rd movement	lift backward and turn to medium level (*i.e.*, spiralling)
4th movement	return to high starting position

This can be performed with a definite indication of one side leading, or symmetrically even. Steps, jumps and travelling to other places in the room can be introduced.

Introduction to movement study and teaching

II

WHEN you have watched someone making a speech, or two people having a conversation, it is likely that you will have seen some hundreds of hand and arm movements which have no external functional use such as picking up an object, but are made in support of words and expressions which are spoken. These *gestures* tell us a great deal about the person and, apart from obvious differences of, say, flamboyant movements and timid one (effort quality variations), two distinct kinds can be recognised. There are those which start near the body and move outwards like the spokes of a wheel from the centre, as might be made with a finger pointing, or conversely those which approach the centre from some distance away. Those movements with a *spoke-like* character are in direct contrast with others which seem to *surround* or *travel around* the body with more sweeping movements. The gesture of indicating an object some distance away can be made in either way.

Rest your hand on the table in front of you, or on the arm of your chair, and, with a movement leading from the back of your hand, point out an object to your right with a gesture which could sweep past if not arrested there, in which case this would be a typical movement around the body. Now withdraw the pointing hand by pulling it in directly towards the body, thus bending the joints of the arm and hand. Repeat this movement a few times to experience the contrast between the "spoke-like" and "edge" or "surrounding" movement. The whole movement might be far extended or very near to the body but the difference between these two fundamental uses of the space around the body is clear.

Recognise the combination of these two uses of space in, for instance, swimming the breast stroke. The arms and legs are used symmetrically to propel the body along. The main action of *pulling* in the arms is a movement surrounding the body from being extended far ahead, while the recovery is a spoke-like gathering-in towards the body, followed by a penetrating of space ahead and away from the body, also spoke-like. The legs also have the combined use of spoke-like and surrounding action.

Some everyday actions are, by their nature, spoke-like. In eating for instance, whatever flourishes or variations in pathway the lifting hand takes, the ultimate object is to reach the mouth and this will never be successfully achieved in making a movement circling around the body. The movement accompanying or achieving the swinging of a scarf round the neck, or a cloak over the shoulders, is an obvious circling or covering around the body.

In primitive fighting actions, the attacking, penetrating action of piercing has its response in a covering, protective attitude. The classical dance forms of arabesque and attitude have just these different uses of space which distinguish them.

USING THIS EXPERIENCE TO STIMULATE CREATIVE MOVEMENT

Examples of the exploratory approach

Freely close in the limbs near to the body, bend in the arms, crouch down to bend in the legs and contrast this with shooting the limbs away from the body centre. Such ideas can be developed in standing and also in positions where weight is supported on other body parts – the seat, the back, the front, one side and so on.

Variations of this spoke-like movement come about if only one limb moves, instead of the whole body, or if one is stressed and made more important than the others. Sequences of one limb followed by another and then another can be made and contrasted with all "spoking" in or out together. A natural parallel is seen in group work, where each person, as a member of the group (just as each limb is a member of the body), moves away from, and towards, a common centre like the spokes of a wheel, either at the same time or one after another. Different levels and the variety of quality with which the movements are made help to clarify the initial play exploration towards a dance form, for instance, shooting out high and creeping back down to the centre, and so on.

In both the individual exploration and in the group work, the repetition of the movement may be exactly similar, or may grow

Introduction to movement study and teaching

or shrink in size and extension over phrases of movement, so building a real sequence or sentence. So an exaggerated extension might naturally necessitate an elevation and jump, and the smaller extension movement only a little way from the body. In the first exaggeration more freedom is experienced than in the restricted extension, and such contrasts are valuable.

Similarly, the wrapping or enveloping of the body or of parts of the body by other parts (most easily the limbs) can be experienced freely with similar variations as for the spoke-like movements.

In combining the two ideas, contrasts can be used such as partner action and response, like a mimed duel: one shoots out, say with the hand leading, towards the partner's feet. The partner responds by a wrapping, covering action of the attacked part, maybe by the other leg, maybe by an arm.

Many traditional folk dances are based on the group idea of surrounding a common centre, *i.e.*, circling, or approaching and withdrawing from the centre. Travelling forward, backward, sideways, lifting and sinking should be freely encouraged, as well as variations of rhythm, provided the main challenge and aim is retained.

Dance exercise approach

Dance exercises can be made, for example, in which spoke-like and enveloping movements are related to specific areas of space with chosen body parts.

1st movement	through the centre of the body from high to medium to open sideways
2nd movement	around the centre of the body, from sideways, over front, to other side behind and to side open (a whole horizontal circle)
3rd movement	transition to starting place, lifted high

Many variations will result from changing the rhythmical phrasing for such a sequence. The children could work together in small groups or with a partner, formulating their chosen rhythms, and arranging the pattern and relationships between each other.

CHAPTER 5

Stopping the flow of movement resulting in different shapes of the body

WHILE we live at all, movement can never wholly stop, but in resting and relaxation the minimum of movement occurs and in sleep all conscious movement ceases. There are other times when we pause or stop and are very conscious of an effort to retain the pause and in this way there is in fact a great deal of movement in the body to hold that position. What does stop is the flow of the body movement through space. In everyday life, this is happening continuously. You walk to a chair and sit down; for a time, longer or shorter, your movement may pause, while you sit in the chair, but it may continue while you restlessly shift and change position. We can consider pauses or stops simply as arrested movement. Try this out, by moving across the room and suddenly stopping your "flow of movement" so that you hold a position, like a still picture taken from a movie. What is interesting in this case is that a high degree of concentration is necessary to keep this position and that if one does so the intention of the previous and subsequent movements can be recognised. By contrast, a pause may arise through the introduction of a new movement which cuts across the previous flow, like the moment when a sudden new thought strikes someone and a momentary (or long) new position intersects the previous flow. For instance, a man might be pacing up and down, deep in thought, head down, and suddenly jerk his head high as the solution to his problem "hits" him.

If we look at a person who holds a position or whose flow of

Introduction to movement study and teaching

movement is interrupted (unless there is complete relaxation), definite tendencies can be seen. The body assumes a certain shape (other than its natural physical build) and these shapes can be determined and clearly differentiated. The man with the sudden solution to his problem might be so uplifted in that moment that he stretches himself high and straight, like a pillar or arrow shape to the ceiling, as though piercing through the space above him. Another person might sit talking to a colleague also in an upright "pin-like" position with elbows drawn into the sides, and legs and feet precisely placed side by side. This "arrow," "pin," "pillar"-like shape of the body is not dependent upon body build; a large, broad person can achieve this elongated lengthening and narrowness equally well.

Try making this shape in your body position and you will recognise that a certain inner or mental attitude results; for some, a familiar attitude, for others an unfamiliar experience. It is not difficult therefore to recognise that the positioning of the body into various shapes is the result of the mental attitude of the person at that moment, and it is not just a haphazard occurrence. What is tasteful to one person may be disliked by another.

If you observe a group of people together, you will be able to distinguish other shapes assumed by the body. Someone might be sitting rounded over, curled almost into a ball-like shape, spine curved around the body centre. Try to make this shape freely in your own position, and perhaps you can recognise how this orientation around the centre of your body gives a quite different experience from the previous shape of elongation. Make these two shapes in sequence: elongate like an arrow, then round like a ball, and repeat this sequence several times.

In making observations of people in everyday life, try to distinguish and select these shapes from others.

USING THIS EXPERIENCE TO STIMULATE MOVEMENT: AN EXPLORATORY APPROACH

The idea that pausing in movement is as important as the activity or "flow of movement" is one which many people fail

Stopping the flow of movement

to realise, so that activity continues without interruption, and the clear statements of meaning get lost. It is like a story written entirely without commas, full stops and paragraphs, so that the clarity is dimmed. The mastery of the moments of pausing can be achieved with children in a play-like way. Using the idea of "stills" from a moving picture, frozen shapes or statues can all help the child to concentrate on this. The traditional game of "statues" is of course based on this simple idea of a whirling flow of movement (where two people spin around together) breaking into a decreasing flow and stopping in a statue. An example of a simple idea which can be used is travelling freely by walking, rolling, or any chosen way of locomotion, and interrupting the travelling at a given moment, as though frozen (a signal can be given by the teacher or chosen by the individual child). The contrasting use of the stop to break and cut through the flow of movement with a new idea can be stimulated by giving a specific task to be achieved in the order: "hands touching the floor," "head high in the air," etc. Specific practice of the definite body shapes – like a pointed arrow or pin, like a ball (small and hard, or large and light, etc.) – should be incorporated in the movement training, and can be used as a challenge for the stopping position.

Dance exercise approach

Here is an example of a sequence, with suggested movements. Try other variations of shape at different levels:

Starting position	like a ball, curled up
1st movement	lift to high elongated position, pause
2nd movement	curve and sink sideways, ending in a round shape
3rd movement	roll over and round to floor
4th movement	shoot outwards with arrow-like shape along the floor
End	pause

In continuing to observe the different body attitudes (and therefore mental attitudes), other fundamental positions and shapes can be recognised.

Introduction to movement study and teaching

Stand with feet apart, elbows sideways and the whole body broadened out to each side. The body assumes a flat "wall-like" position, and has the characteristic of dividing or separating the space into two parts, the area in front from the area behind. Recollect in movement the two previous shapes discussed above: the arrow-like elongation and the ball-like rounding. Each has

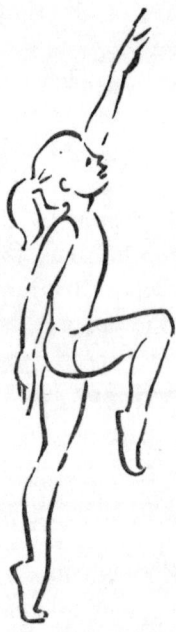

Fig. 4 Arrow-like position

its own characteristic movement: the arrow which shoots or penetrates through space, and the ball which moves with a rolling action around a centre. A fourth shape, that of a twist, can also be recognised. Such a twisted shape has two or more counter-directional tendencies with different parts of the body, quite different from the single-centre focus of the ball-like shape.

Try out for yourself these different positions:

(a) The thin, arrow-like position, where all parts of the body

Stopping the flow of movement

"line up" into a single length as far as this is possible in the body. This need not be only in the up/down direction but the point of the arrow can be directed to any place – diagonally, horizontally, etc. A supporting leg stance need not detract from the experience of the arrow-like position (*see* Fig. 4).

(*b*) The round, ball-like position, where all parts of the body collect round a centre, near and tight, or further away and larger. The centre can be at the front of the body, standing,

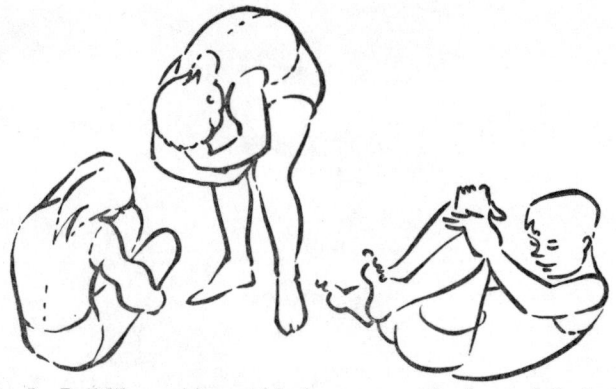

Fig. 5 Ball-like positions, with the centre at the front of the body

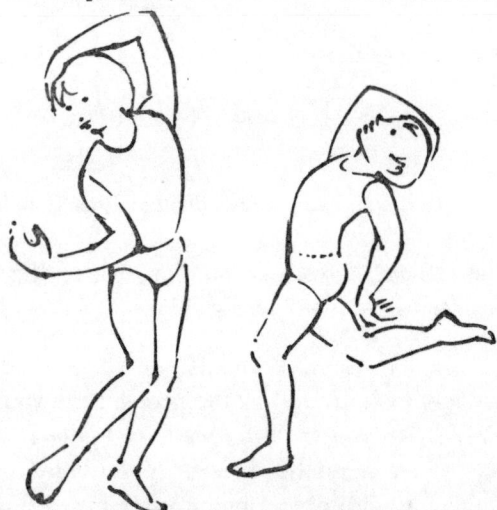

Fig. 6 (*left*) Ball-like position, with the centre at the side of the body   Fig. 7 (*right*) Ball-like position, with the centre at the back of the body

Introduction to movement study and teaching

sitting or lying on the back (*see* Fig. 5); it can be at the side (*see* Fig. 6) or at the back (*see* Fig. 7).

(*c*) The flat, wall-like position, where the body forms a broad flat shape. It can divide front from back (*see* Fig. 8), high from low (*see* Fig. 9) or side from side (*see* Fig. 10).

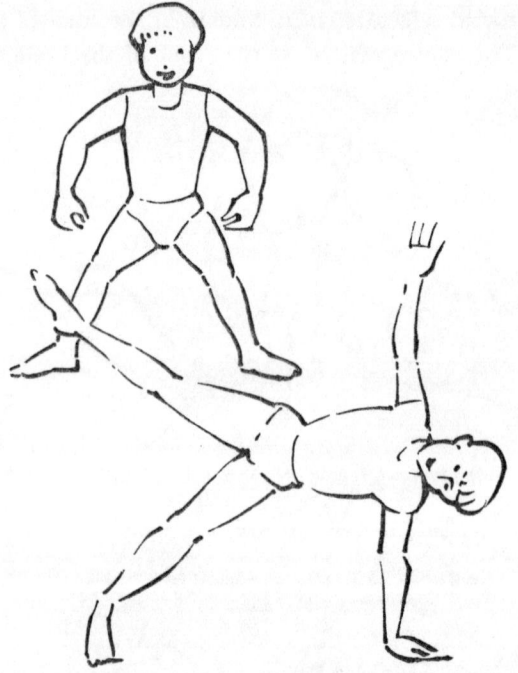

Fig. 8   Flat, wall-like position, dividing front from back

(*d*) The twisted, screw-like position, where the body parts face in counter-directions (*see* Fig. 11).

Observe these in everyday life. If you sit in a restaurant or railway carriage, look around at the people near you; some will most certainly strike you as "pure wall" or "pure twist," etc., as they sit. But others may well present a combined mixture, for instance, a pin top with a wall bottom (*see* Fig. 12) or a twisted pin (*see* Fig. 13).

Stopping the flow of movement

Try to observe many of these and to write them down, in words or sketches.

It has already been hinted that these shapes which the body assumes have certain characteristic movements and are not only

Fig. 9 (*left*) Flat, wall-like position, dividing high from low (horizontal)

Fig. 10 (*right*) Flat, wall-like position, dividing side from side

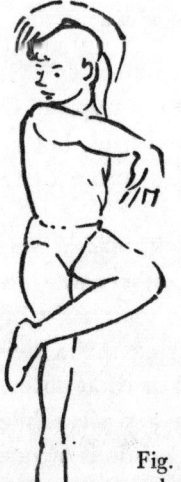

Fig. 11 Twisted, screw-like shape in upright position

Introduction to movement study and teaching

static positions. In this sense, movement can be thought of as constantly changing positions, sometimes with a pause, but frequently like a film going through thousands of still pictures which, when run one after the other, give the illusion of movement. Each "still" is only a fraction of a position different from the previous and subsequent pictures.

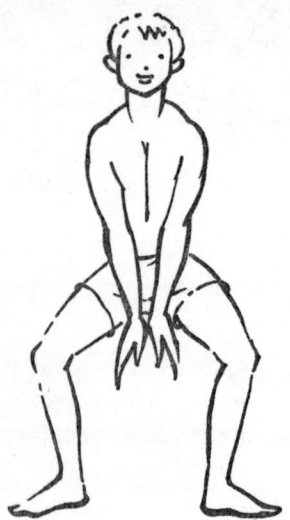

Fig. 12 (*left*) A pin top with a wall bottom   Fig. 13 (*right*) A twisted pin

Now try to observe these typical body shapes not only in position when movement is held, but also in action. The movement we make when going into a cartwheel is wall-shaped (*see* Fig. 14).

In walking, some people hold a very still, upright position, stressing the up or down, others sway from side to side, stressing the broad wall-like shape, some twist hips or shoulders in slinky counter-movements, bringing out a twisted shape of the body, while others might round or droop over. Watch different people to see this. If the person also sits while you are observing, see whether the same characteristic is obvious in the pause or rest as in the walk, or for instance whether the person with a tendency

Stopping the flow of movement

to mince along like an upright pillar droops and rounds like a ball when he sits. Again there are obvious mixtures of shapes.

In everyday life these various attitudes have a practical significance and use: the broad, steady, wall-like attitude of the policeman keeping back the crowd (*e.g.*, separating the crowd from the roadway), the twisting in and out of the person getting

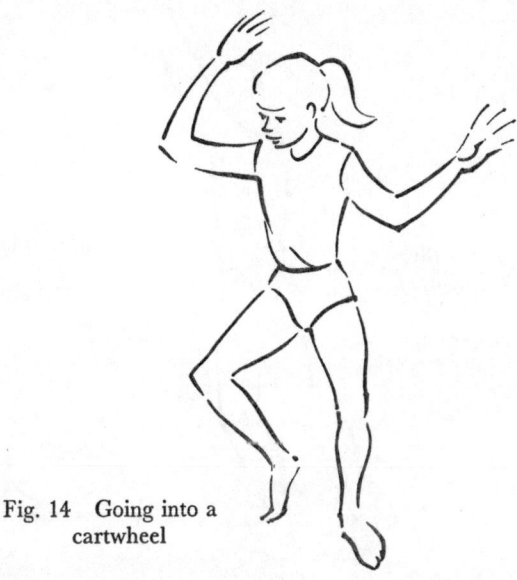

Fig. 14 Going into a cartwheel

through a crowd of people (avoiding and going around obstacles), the upright elongation to peer over someone's head or the curling up of the body to get through a small low opening. These are not reflections of personality, but rather the practical use of the body.

USING THIS EXPERIENCE TO STIMULATE MOVEMENT: AN EXPLORATORY APPROACH

(*a*) A class can experience the different inner reactions to making various definite body shapes. It is probably best to begin with clear and simple shapes, rather than combined ones. Imaginative words like those used earlier often help to stimulate the achievement of the shape formation quickly. Variation of shapes should be attempted in all positions (not only in standing), at different extensions, *e.g.*, small, hard ball, lighter, larger one, short arrow, one which seems to elongate beyond the ends of fingers and toes, etc.

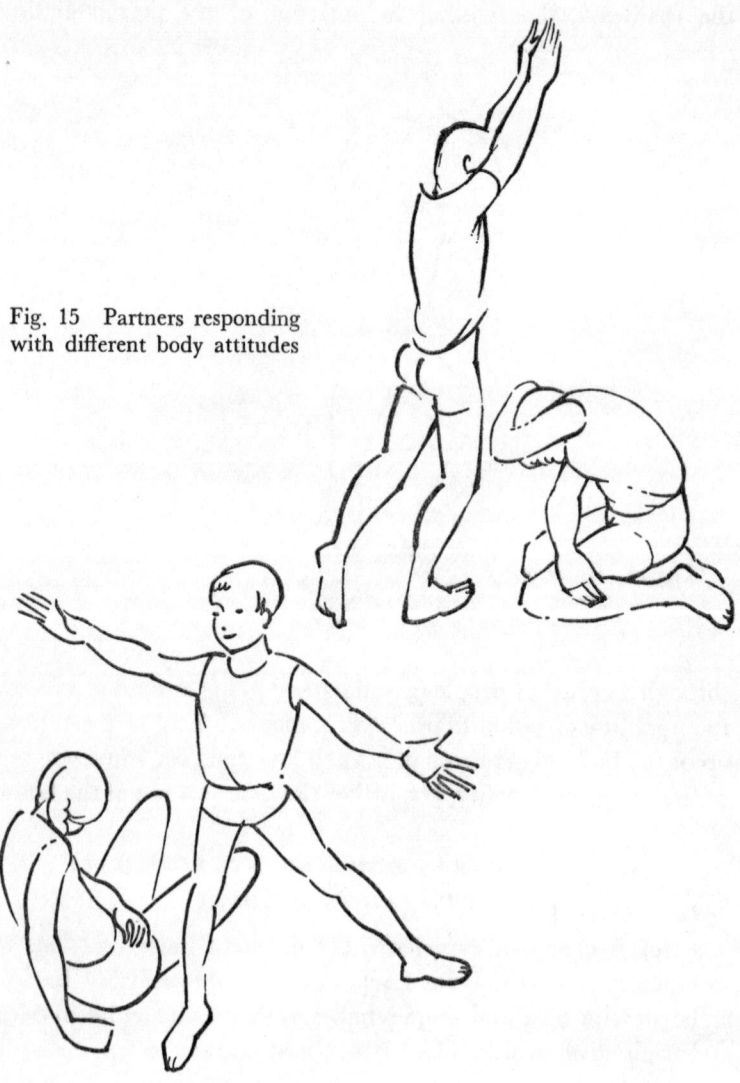

Fig. 15 Partners responding with different body attitudes

Stopping the flow of movement

(*b*) The encouraging of observation of these shapes by the class can be done by working with a partner: A chooses and makes his shape, B watches and responds with a different one (or the same one, or the same but in a different position, etc., as the task may vary). Only one idea of response should be presented at the one time (*see* Fig. 15).

(*c*) Choosing a series of shapes and moving between them. One example might be starting rounded and small, growing

Fig. 16   Arrow group

into an arrow, as though it shoots out of the middle of the ball, which then melts into a twisted, screwed-up shape or gets broken and jagged, forming a twisted shape with an angular pattern. In a sequence of these changing shapes, a rhythmical development of the movement should be encouraged. Usually a free rhythm will develop naturally if the sequence is repeated a few times in the same way. Help can be given towards this if necessary by suggesting, for instance, that the arrow might shoot out very far and quickly, poise for a second and then break in sudden jerks.

(*d*) A hint of ideas for group movement and formation can be made here. Similar group shapes are possible, where the "body" is a few people (just as an individual body has many

Introduction to movement study and teaching

parts), *e.g.*, a group like an arrow with one person as a point and the others behind. In this case, each member of the group might not in fact assume a full "arrow-like" shape in his own body, but would contribute to the complete shape of the group. For instance, for the group to dive down from a height into a deep position, those at the front may finish kneeling or flat down while those at the back might still be high (*see* Fig. 16).

Fig. 17 Ball group

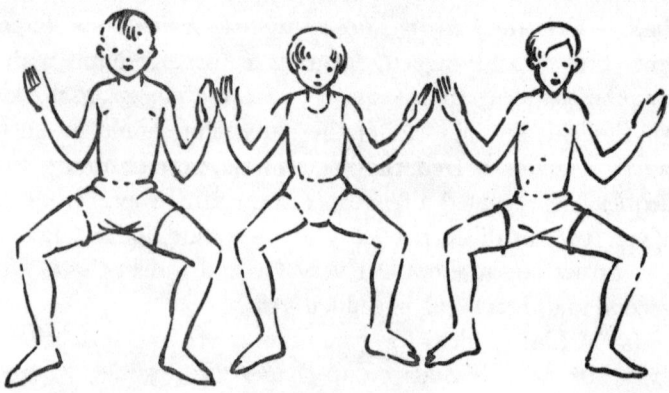

Fig. 18 Wall group

Stopping the flow of movement

Fig. 19 Weaving in and out

Fig. 20 A attacks

Introduction to movement study and teaching

Similarly a rounded group of people might form a solid group, like a ball around one centre or curved over each other (*see* Fig. 17).

A wall or flat group may be any number deep, extended far, or squeezed close (*see* Fig. 18). Or a group could twist amongst itself, weaving in and out (*see* Fig. 19).

Fig. 21   B curls away

Dramatic movement group plays (just as individuals playing together) can be built up of action and reaction, like the arrow piercing and breaking through the wall, dividing it into two parts which roll away (like balls) separately and rejoin as an arrow to face the original one, and so on.

(*e*) Clarification of dramatic characters or caricatures can be assisted by the study of the fundamental body attitudes or shapes. Many scenes with different character types can be

Stopping the flow of movement

Fig. 22   A curls, surrounding B

Fig. 23   B twists away, escapes and establishes the first broad position

Introduction to movement study and teaching

Fig. 24   A retires, curled into a ball

built, and a certain simplification can be achieved by this means.

Example of action and reaction of partners

    First action : A attacks (*see* Fig. 20).
    Reaction   : B curls away (*see* Fig. 21).
    New action : A curls, surrounding B (*see* Fig. 22).
    Reaction   : B twists away, escapes and establishes the first broad position (*see* Fig. 23).
               A retires, curled into a ball (*see* Fig. 24).

CHAPTER 6

The balance of the weight of the body

IF you stand on both feet, exaggeratedly even, with feet apart, you can achieve a very stable and firm position, which is rooted to the ground. Upon this solid basis, most of our everyday actions happen and the ability to retain this stability is one of the things which young children strive for in learning to walk and stand. Observe very young children standing and walking – they find it difficult to balance on the comparatively small base of two feet and it is quite advanced for a baby to stand with feet close together. It is even more difficult for him to keep the alternation of taking weight on one foot, then the other, in walking. The instability frequently results in a fall or tumble to the ground where a larger base and more solid hold can be maintained.

Compare for yourself this balance and stability with the instability and off-balance which occurs if you lean away from the support of your feet, throwing your weight off its stable support. In this case, you have to move away from the spot unless you wish to fall down like the baby. This off-balance leaning cannot be maintained in a position or shape, but results in a flow of movement.

Watch a group of people together and observe how they sit. Some will be upright or broad and very stable, firmly balanced on the chair. Others will be leaning over, dependent upon some outside support to keep them from toppling over; take away the chair arm, the table or wall, and they would be unable to retain their position.

In locomotion, both bodily expressions (*i.e.*, of the stable and

Introduction to movement study and teaching

held position, and the leaning or changing) are possible. Compare the solid pacing of some adults with the more fluent off-balance running of many children at play. The tendency towards the static on the one hand, and more fluid positions and movements on the other hand can be observed, even when the extremes do not occur. In standing, the constantly changing swing-over from one foot to the other when the whole body weight shifts across or around gives the person restless but adjustable situations, a series of positions which are *en route* to a new place, and from which a quick and adaptable change can be achieved. It is much more difficult to make a quick adaptation to a demand to move (*e.g.*, to avoid something) for the person who is firmly rooted to the ground on both feet.

The combinations of movement qualities which result in these two clearly contrasting movement happenings can in their extremes be described as continuity in flow and time (like the excess and lack of control seen in the movement of a drunk person) and static positioning and held shapes (like someone who is immovable and solid as a rock). This gives a hint towards the relationship of the bodily attitudes and the accompanying mental states. If the actor portrays a character in extreme agitation – one who is panic-stricken and unable to make a sensible action – he might choose to dash here and there, with almost uncontrolled changes of direction, lacking any stability and poise, or stand stock-still, like a hypnotised rabbit, rooted to the spot, unable to make any adjustment. Both reactions would be possible, but would be characteristic of two different kinds of person.

USING THIS EXPERIENCE TO STIMULATE MOVEMENT: AN EXPLORATORY APPROACH

(*a*) Practise balancing the weight of the body on different parts of the body, so that a stable, held position (and shape) is achieved. In stepping, keep the body upright and balanced immediately over the new stance; it probably helps at first to give a pause between each step and a regular rhythm. The rest of the body should balance freely, to help the stability of the position.

The balance and weight of the body

(*b*) Stand with feet together and lean over away from stance, letting the weight take you away from the spot, dropping or reeling about freely. Then bring in a lighter control, resist the heavy dropping, and try to catch the weight without flopping, continuing the flow of movement, perhaps with poised turns in order to keep on the feet before travelling away again. Freely let this movement develop into rolls and poising high off the ground with continuous flow.

(*c*) In the air, swing the whole body diagonally off the ground and fly into space, catching the weight, only to swing backwards towards the floor.

(*d*) Contrast this with jumping in the air where a definite position of the body is achieved and held, say upright and straight.

(*e*) Contrast these stable and off-balance movements freely in a sequence (which can gradually be repeated and remembered to encourage memory of performed movement).

(*f*) Different character types can be developed through the study of these contrasting body attitudes, *e.g.*, a sailor's walk (off-balance, easily adjusting to changing floor tilts), stolid farmer's walk (down to earth), etc.

Sequence for whole body action

Starting position	high and stable
1st movement	move to low and stable
2nd movement	lean high into diagonal and travel from spot
3rd movement	lower from height, still moving
4th movement	catch weight firmly over feet, stable
End	pause

Allow a natural, rhythmical development, either for the whole class in unison, or for each child or group to formulate on its own.

CHAPTER 7

The body draws shapes in the surrounding space

An aspect of movement which can easily be seen by an observer is the shape which the moving limb or part of the body makes as it changes from one action to another. The action may be a functional one, like handling objects as in a factory job, or it may be an expressive gesture, made while describing something or in support of a verbal statement.

At first, watch movements made as functional or working actions: someone washing up, cleaning a room, putting on a coat, or making something, or a child handling and playing with a toy. With some people, the air patterns which are drawn will be very clear, and you will be able to reproduce them easily – even write them down (*see* Fig. 25).

Fig. 25   Air patterns

With others, you might find greater difficulty in recognising any clear shapes, and notice only that a haphazard vagueness appears. If this is habitual, you would not expect such people to be very expert in manual precision work. In observing working actions, many of the shapes used are directly related to the particular material. For instance, a curved shape might arise

Body shapes

because the hand has to avoid a piece of machinery. But even so, there are many intermediate movements which are not influenced by the manipulating of material, and which reveal individual variations. If two people make the same sequence of actions in a job, the main actions may be similar, but the general pattern, shape and rhythm will doubtless be different, even though the two may be equally efficient. It is not necessarily true that the shortest and most obvious route or shape is the most efficient for everyone. Some people will choose a variation which might appear less simple but which will suit their individual make-up better. Only if the result is less efficient than it might be should any alteration be attempted.

Such personal movement shapes can be clearly seen in a person's expressive actions. Just as the individual choice and

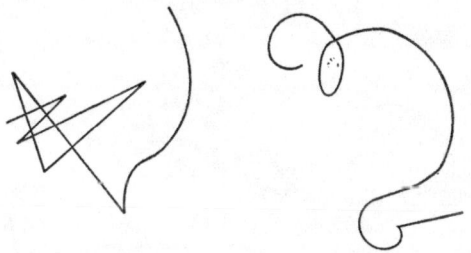

Fig. 26 Two-gesture patterns

variation of, say, stress and accent, or of body shape, or of stable balance as against mobile, is significant of personality, so the shape choice is also important.

Look at two people talking together, and try to distinguish the shape patterns which they use in their gestures and what the different choice of each is (*see* Fig. 26).

When you have written down these free patterns, you will see that many are combined shapes, but there are really only three basic ones:

    1. A round shape, *i.e.*, a shape which continually repeats itself in the same curve. It may grow or shrink in size, or become elongated into a spiral but it retains this basic principle (*see* Fig. 27).

Introduction to movement study and teaching

Fig. 27 Three shapes based on a repeated curve

2. A shape which reverses its direction and makes a twist like a letter S (*see* Fig. 28). To show this on paper is to deprive it of its three-dimensional quality, in contrast with a simple circle which remains in one plane.

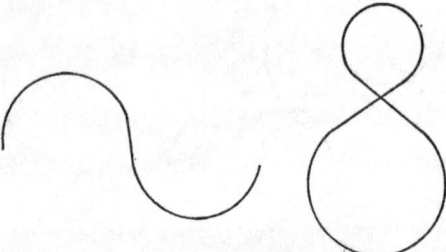

Fig. 28 Two twisted shapes

3. An angular shape, the character of which is its immediate change from one direction into a new direction (*see* Fig. 29).

Fig. 29 An angular shape

Body shapes

Make these patterns for yourself, at first singly, then combining two and then all three together. Try to recognise those which feel more familiar to you and those which are strange.

A combined functional and expressive action which gives easy scope for observation is the act of smoking. With such an automatised action, the main stress is on expressive movement (except with the beginner smoker). The patterns which different people make in this simple movement, taking a cigarette from hand to mouth and back, are very illuminating. Some shapes are shown in Fig. 30 and many flourishes and adornments are added during conversation.

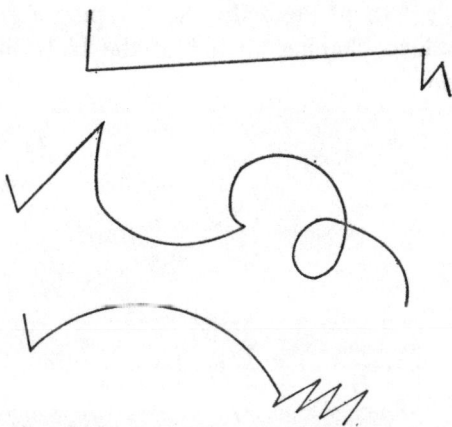

Fig. 30   Three examples of air patterns made while smoking

USING THIS EXPERIENCE TO STIMULATE MOVEMENT

The free drawing of shapes in the air around the body is frequently used by the infant teacher who tries to help the pupils to recognise and draw letters and numbers. This developing shape sense of the child is helped by playing with bricks of different sizes and shapes and it is rather in this three-dimensional way that the feeling for shapes in the body can be experienced. The growing and shrinking of a simple shape – say a rounding – should be developed as a rhythmical sequence, which might extend far into space at the largest extension, and be a tiny body movement at its smallest.

Introduction to movement study and teaching

The development in floor patterns can well be studied in connection with drawing air patterns, for there is a natural link between resulting floor patterns and the shape of the movement which the body makes. For instance, an angular movement drawn high in the air, forward, would probably result in a jump, landing at a new position in front of the previous one. A circular movement taken in even increasing extension would naturally lead to a floor pattern echoing the air pattern. This should be taken from the successive leaning of the body weight into different directions.

Freely exploring the drawing of shapes in the air, which then can be fixed exactly in directions in space, should be made with many different parts of the body: legs shaping a gesture before stepping, shoulders shaping an arc as the body lifts from the floor, and so on.

CHAPTER 8

The lesson

ALTHOUGH there are no "rules" for the planning of a lesson, a good working basis is achieved by the selection of contrasting ideas. Rarely, if ever, will there be occasion for retaining throughout a lesson the same unrelieved idea (this would be counter to the "activity and recovery" theme of Chapter 3).

What these contrasting ideas might be and some of the ways in which they can be stimulated will be discussed here.

The immediate aims should be:

    to give opportunity for spontaneous movement and dance;

    to give opportunity for taking part in others' movement compositions (children's or the teacher's);

    to encourage the composition of movement and dance ideas by the class, by repetition and by selection.

All can be either:

individual
with a partner
with a small group
with a large group.

The balance between the suggestions above will be according to the age and needs of the particular class at any time. This can be understood as a general and educational need, and the way in which the teacher selects the right material stimulus for the class, together with the students' ability to build and develop the growing movement ideas and experiences, will determine the educational value of the work with the class.

Introduction to movement study and teaching

Mention will be made in the following chapters of:
   using percussion instruments
   using imagery for stimulating action
   group movement
   movement, colour and pattern.

The use of music will not be dealt with in great detail in this book but reference should be made to *Listen and Move* records available from Macdonald & Evans. For help in specific choice of music and in improvisation, teachers will find the following useful: the chapter "Music for Modern Educational Dance" in *Music and Physical Education* by R. M. Thachray, *Modern Dance Accompaniment* by Adda Heynssen and all Dance and Movement publications from Macdonald & Evans.

Briefly, then, music, improvised or composed according to need, can be used in different ways:

Dance which follows exactly the construction of the music (*e.g.*, a fugue), which has a shape emphasis, and has the same theme repeated. This might suggest different people moving, or different groups; one person following the theme might have the main movement, while others accompany with smaller movements.

Dance based primarily on the mood or feeling of the music, *e.g.*, *Largo* (Heynssen).

Dance which reacts to the stimulus to action and rhythm, *e.g.*, *Tango* (Heynssen) and many national dances.

Music as background to dance or drama, to help characterising (the obvious example could be quoted of piano accompaniment to melodramas), to set a scene and general mood where the precise rhythms and phrases may not be followed exactly, *e.g.*, sea music, Chinese street scene, etc. Even if the music is not followed as closely as in the above examples, the movements of climax, change, increase, decrease and pauses should be clearly defined to help the dramatic effect of excitement, anticipation, explosion, etc.

Much of the work in the art of movement will include

The lesson

movement sequences and dances to which the music is added later, or to which there is no music at all.

THE TEACHER'S ROLE

What is the teacher's role in taking a movement lesson? We must distinguish between material (the principles and ideas about movement as an art) and method of presentation.

Too often, there is a belief that the method of presentation involves "doing what you choose," "freedom" and "individuality." So it does, and all these are important in the education of children, but there is the balance to this: "doing what is prescribed, accurately and well," "discipline" and "group awareness." It is in balancing these two sides that the art of movement can play an important part in education.

The "exploratory" and "formal" methods of teaching are not exclusively right or wrong and certainly the material can be presented either way. In my opinion, generally the exploratory approach for art of movement experience is suitable for some of the work in primary schools and for first-year secondary children. But even so, it would be very advantageous for children to have interspersed, as needed, moments of "formal" teaching, to help them over a sticky patch, to enlarge their range and to stretch them further.

By the secondary stage, I believe that art of movement training should arise from the needs of the dance or drama, that composed forms of both (by the children or teacher) should be achieved, and that too much labouring of "exploring" the possibilities of movement becomes tedious. In any event, exploration comes through a definite response to movement challenges and the choice of challenge must vary according to the experience of the class, the age and general stage of maturity and development. A good teacher will find ways of presentation for the most simple ideas, without offending the very sensitive dignity of the adolescent.

The teacher must be adaptable and able to vary his relationship with the class at a particular time. To stand in the centre of the

Introduction to movement study and teaching

room, with the class around, is a wise teaching situation (as long as you remember to turn round) as the children are fairly equally dispersed in relation to you. It gives a psychological advantage in setting the spirit of the class as a unit and a focus inside the group. But it is necessary to withdraw from the group, to take away that focus, when you expect the class to work alone, individually or in groups, to disappear to the edge of the room, or to move unobtrusively from one area to another. There may also be some occasions when the teacher literally leads a group or even stands in front of a class to instruct.

Is demonstration good? Yes, and no. Yes, if an exact movement is being taught, is being observed and copied by the class (this happens frequently with older secondary children when a formal or set dance is being "polished"). Yes, if the teacher wishes to inspire the class with the mood, spirit and wide scope of response to a movement challenge. This would necessitate demonstrating a dozen variations of the possible responses to a challenge. The children should not copy these, nor remain under the impression that there is "nothing to do." No, if the demonstration is limited, poor, or restrictive.

The use of the voice by the teacher is of importance in so far as it reflects his inner participation. It can, used well, be a source of inspiration and stimulus to a class. It should not be the exclusive stimulus, nor be too repetitively used. Consciously withdrawing the emotional excitement from the intonation of the voice can be refreshing for the class.

THE BEGINNING OF A LESSON

This should set the mood and general attitude of the class to what it is going to do. Simple repetitive movement can hold and concentrate attention, for it is often unreasonable to expect a class or group coming into a hall or space to be immediately inventive and co-operative. Where possible, the introductory activities should be related to the lesson either by practising movements later to be used, or by the use of deliberate contrast. A

The lesson

knowledge of how different movements can stimulate different states of mind will be of immense value. The aim should be a freeing of tension and a concentration and absorption in action. An experienced teacher will know the effect created by the different movement happenings. The inexperienced teacher would be well advised to observe and record the results which arise, and to try to distinguish the effects on the class of the movement itself, the teacher's own manner of presentation, the tempo, and the accompaniment, if any is used. The teacher must be ready to direct the rhythmical phrase and accent. It is from his own practice, previous to the lesson, that the teacher can find out the necessary rhythmical phrases of any given movement sequence. It is through accurate observation that any adaptation of this prearranged rhythm can spontaneously be achieved.

All of the following suggestions for action are well known in everyday life for warming up and a selection from these would be useful in teaching older primary children.

Rubbing and shaking

If our hands are cold it is easy and natural to rub them or shake them to stimulate the circulation. The same treatment can be applied to the rest of the body. To rub the back of a partner not only warms the back, but also the person administering the action. Shaking relaxed hands from the wrists in different directions – up and down, side to side, round and round – is a simple movement sequence for the group and should be performed in rhythmical phrases. It will be less easy for the group to perform a similar shaking of the feet from the ankle, and this might need many weeks of work and repetition before the same relaxed letting-go can be achieved. It sometimes helps to grip above the ankle with both hands and to try to relax the foot while activating the movement from the hands (in a sitting position). Relaxed shaking of the shoulders can help to loosen a stiff upper body, but again can prove difficult to a beginner in movement. Not too long should be spent in improving this during each lesson, for simple repetition will gradually affect the performance.

Large body action of swinging

Relaxed swinging movements, supported by a resilient or "spongy" leg action, are both pleasing and easy to perform. Transferring the weight of the body from one leg to the other in a side to side action can be the beginning of a more mobile stance, and the easy rhythm of the swing makes this smooth and flowing. The gradual emphasis of the hip action moving in a U-shape, while keeping the body vertical, mobilises the whole of the lower part of the body, spine, hips, knees and ankles. More interesting movement is achieved by increasing the extension, *i.e.*, making the U-shape larger, and by introducing a lift at the ends of the swing so that the feet are more fully used, until there is a balancing on the ball of the foot at each side. This is a preliminary to a lift or a jump off the ground. Swinging of the upper part of the body backwards and forwards, from side to side or diagonally can be introduced and should not be too isolated. Where the aim of the movement is mobilising and warming, there is no special value in keeping the legs rigid and stiff. The more the whole body is incorporated, the more effective the movement. Leg swinging with a resilient supporting leg action can be first performed in the easiest directions of forward and backward, and later across the body and to the side, and diagonally crossing and open. Holding hands with a partner, or in a circle, for support will help. It will be necessary to practise resilient leg support: a simple bouncing on both legs, then on one and then on the other. The rhythmical increase and decrease of the size of the extension of the swing will add interest and provide a natural recovery. For instance, one sequence could progress from small to medium to large and to very far extension in a series of phrases, four groups of three beats each. The larger movement will be either much faster, or the music must take longer. Continuous action and a natural resilient recovery can be achieved, by changing from one leg to the other during the phrase, for older children, *e.g.*, swinging right leg forward, backward, forward, backward, change legs, and left leg forward, backward, forward, backward, change legs. Rhythmical bouncing on

The lesson

both legs in between the group of swings can give a transition or the swing can be transferred immediately from one leg to the other. Simple arc swings, like a pendulum, and, as a development after these are mastered, circling and figure of eight swings can be introduced. The clarity of the shape should be emphasised and recognition made of the stress and recovery part of the shape, *i.e.*, the stress on the drop, or the accent on the lift.

Stretching or tension, and recovery in relaxation

The early morning yawning which often accompanies a stretching and tensing of muscles is naturally followed by a recovery of heaviness and a pleasant relaxed feeling. A similar experience may be gained at the beginning of a session by a slow, exaggerated extension of the limbs and spine, holding the position for a moment and an immediate relaxation with a semi-collapse. A rhythmical alternation of the tension (or extension) and the relaxing will help to carry the movement on, and avoid the danger of a lethargic flop. The body should be considered either as one whole unit as above, or in parts. For instance special attention may be advantageously applied to the neck and shoulder area, or to the sides of the body, or to the legs and feet. A gradual awareness of the different muscle groups will result from such concentration on specific areas.

Travelling in the room

There is a mental as well as physical stimulus in changing position. Any class where the members stay on the same spot for too long is likely to become over-static and dull. Special care should be taken in establishing good habits of stepping and foot placement. When the feet are warm and eased, stepping can be quickened, and can be changed to easy running, leaping or skipping. Stimulating sound accompaniment can be of great help here. Attention also should be paid to the poise or attitude of the body; for instance, whether the body is held upright or moving from side to side, whether the arms are swinging loosely or held still, and so on. Repetitive sequences of travelling round a room can be used, or end to end.

CHAPTER 9

Using percussion instruments

USING PERCUSSION INSTRUMENTS TO ACCOMPANY MOVEMENT

A RHYTHMIC, percussive sound is felt by most people as a potent stimulus to move; it might be only a jigging up and down, or a whole-hearted (and -bodied) jive. Primitive peoples recognise and use the inate rhythmic sense in man in developing their rituals and dances, and young children can often be seen tapping or jumping out a rhythmic pattern as they sit or walk about. It is in no way to over-develop the "primitive" side of our natures that percussive sounds and dancing with percussion instruments are used. It is rather a recognition of the two-sidedness of movement (as of sound), and the rhythmic need and enjoyment cannot be denied if we look at the teenager's joy in exciting rhythmical dancing. As music has melody and rhythm, so movement has shape and rhythm. Movement training covers both aspects.

Percussive sounds stimulate the rhythmic sense in movement, and it is not surprising to observe that children develop a feeling for rhythm when quite young; some children enjoy it more than others, of course, but few lack this sense entirely. The drawing and understanding of such shapes is a later development.

For infant and junior children, records of short percussion compositions have been made (Records I and II in the *Listen and Move* series from Macdonald & Evans). These are intended mainly for the teacher who feels a need to give the class a sound stimulus to move and who does not feel able to play the instruments himself. Also some are more complicated than any one person could play alone.

Using percussion instruments

Of the many uses of percussion instruments, let us first discuss playing the instrument for a dancing group, *i.e.*, an outside sound like a record to initiate and to accompany the movement.

It is necessary for the teacher to practise the handling and use of instruments, in order to become confident in their use while teaching and observing. The best way to play any instrument which is easily portable is to make the movement sequence in miniature, "getting the feel" of the movement rhythm and phrase at the time of playing. This will ensure that a purely mechanised rhythm and beat is avoided (unless deliberately chosen).

Some suggestions for the varied movement ideas which can be stimulated through percussive sounds follow:

(*a*) Mainly for older children and young people. A repetitive rhythmical beat, say, 1, 2, 3, 1, 2, 3, in stepping (note that the accent comes on alternating sides). A development of a simple forward step can come through stressing the accent deep (near the ground, or bending the knees), even with a jump into the accented first step. This gives a ländler-type step pattern. Introduce turns and changes of direction, partners meeting, separating or going around and a simple dance is born. A gradual crescendo in speed and strength, and the whole mood and spirit is more lively and gay. Taking the same rhythm, but smoothly, like a waltz, gliding over the floor, gives an entirely different character and quality which can be contrasted in both sound and movement.

The class should be encouraged to make variations of patterns and form, bringing into action the whole body and not only the legs, *e.g.*, with a strong hitting action down into the ground, on the downward jump, or a horizontal gliding action on the smooth stepping. If no action is made with the upper part of the body, a definite body carriage and presence should be achieved, where the retaining of the held position is significant, *e.g.*, arms clasped in front, elbows lifted sideways, or hands linked behind the back.

(*b*) A regular 1, 2, 1, 2, 1, 2 beat, which can even be

recognised by young children. Here the accent is repeatedly on the same side of the body and a more regular marching-type step results.

(c) Combined even and odd accents, *e.g.*, 1, 2, 1, 2, 3/ 1, 2, 1, 2, 3, or 1, 2, 3, 1, 2/1, 2, 3, 1, 2 (five rhythms), 1, 2, 1, 2, 3, 1, 2/1, 2, 1, 2, 3, 1, 2 (a seven-rhythm sequence), are easily experienced in the body when and if such alternating stresses of different sides of the body are recognised; *e.g.*, right, left; right, left, right; left, right, *i.e.*, two accents on the same side, then a change. It is important that such regular time and stress accents are presented to the class through a repeated movement action, and in the first stages a direct counting, or even an intellectual understanding, is not necessary or desirable.

(d) An irregular but phrased and repeated sequence of sounds, *i.e.*, a free rhythm without regular time counting. Such a phrase needs to be repeated accurately many times before the class will feel confident in response, but they should immediately make a movement response. A phrase can be given for the class to choose its own movement reaction, when each person will make an individual sequence, or a suggested movement sequence can be given. For such a phrase, a sequence might be:

> jumping on the first three accents, and a strong hitting action on the last two, with stepping or running on the quick unaccentuated parts, and a long sweeping movement on the smooth continuous sound, *i.e.*, jump, step, step, glide, jump, step, step, jump, step, stamp, stamp.

Variations of direction (*i.e.*, turning, jumping, travelling forward, backward, etc.) and levels of deep down, horizontal or high, give wide scope for variation. The whole phrase could be divided between partners, sometimes one in action while the other holds a position, sometimes both moving simultaneously.

Using percussion instruments

If the teacher (or one of the class) is playing the instrument, it is important that the class feels secure in the sound, that it is accurately repeated and that a developed phrase is given, whether a regular or irregular rhythm. As with music, the ending should be clear and have a logical build-up, either increasing to a climax, decreasing to silence or symmetrically building up a pattern in sound by grouping the phrases, *i.e.*, avoiding a continuous, repetitive beat which soon becomes dull, and then ending the sound without reason.

The choice of instrument varies according to the mood of action it is desired to stimulate, *i.e.*

A drum can be forceful and vigorous, or lighter and sharper if played on the edge with a stick handle or with finger tips.

A gong is obviously useful for an accented movement which smoothly dies away, or an even roll without breaks.

Clappers and castanets give lively staccato accents.

Shakers, maracas and tambourines give a shaking, vibrating stimulus.

These variations are obvious and many sound effects can be obtained from a limited number of instruments if plenty of experiments are made. It is usually important that the teacher chooses instruments which are easily portable, so that he is not restricted to standing in one place in the room, and an ability to play with confidence enables him to observe the class at the same time.

As a contrast to the use of sound to stimulate movement and dance, it is useful to consider the value of accompanying a developed sequence or dance with sound. Here it becomes important both to observe accurately and to choose carefully the sound which will support and not destroy the original movement.

In observing, the following points must be considered :

(*a*) The mood of the action.
(*b*) Its rhythmical development (whether free or regular).

Introduction to movement study and teaching

(c) The build-up of the dance (*e.g.*, when the climax comes).

These three aspects will influence the choice and playing of the instruments. A satisfactory accompaniment takes some time to develop. The teacher should observe carefully that the children who are dancing are not distracted from the movement ideas by poor accompaniment. Attention should be paid to the possibility of voice accompaniment, either alone or in addition to instruments. One of the best introductions to a study of accompaniment is through the use of voice, as stimulus or accompaniment. For young children, the playing of an instrument is quite a complicated affair, but the voice is simple and natural for them.

Try out for yourself, and with a class, if this is possible, how simple sounds stimulate or accompany movement. In the most advanced use of percussion, a whole orchestra can combine, as a musical composition and, of course, in this way, a more complicated sound play is possible.

MOVING AND PLAYING PERCUSSION AT THE SAME TIME

The playing of percussion by a person moving is a quite different experience from those already described. Here, the movement and sound are developed simultaneously. Here are some ideas which can be given to encourage this.

(a) Each member of the group should become familiar with a single instrument by handling it, freely changing the instrument from one hand to the other, tossing it into the air (when safe, both to class and instrument) and attempting to hold and play with different parts of the body (*e.g.*, tapping the tambourine on knees, heels, etc.). This can lead to amusing sequences and playful familiarity with the instrument. It seems to be a necessary introduction to a class which is new to the handling of instruments. For the young child, it is very difficult to master the skill of holding, playing and dancing simultaneously and, for this reason, it is often preferable to leave such percussion work until a certain basic ease and familiarity of movement

Using percussion instruments

has been accomplished. This may apply to older children and adults too but it has also been observed that some classes find that "something to hold on to" gives a certain objectivity to the movement and helps to give them ideas for moving, as well as a focus. This is a somewhat personal affair and depends upon the confidence in presentation. Individual sequences can be achieved and repeated, or this handling stage can be left as a simple exploratory one. For more experienced classes, the idea can be returned to, and then definite dance or movement sequences should be developed.

(b) The shape of the instrument can be used to evoke movement ideas: the fat roundness of a big drum might stimulate rolling and swaying movements, the smallness of an irregular clump of bells might stimulate small refined movements of the hands, feet, knees, etc.

When using a free exploratory approach, it will probably be necessary to give a wide variety of ideas, *e.g.*

(*i*) Let the instrument take you down near the ground (crawling, rolling, crouching, etc.), or high into the air, making you stretch up or jump. Now continue these two ideas, sometimes high, sometimes low.

(*ii*) It might make you whirl round, like a top, or turn very slowly.

(*iii*) Combine (*i*) and (*ii*) into spiralling high and uncurling deep, etc.

(*iv*) It can make you fly out into space, swooping or flying a long way from where you start, trying always to catch up with your instrument, or it can come near to you, becoming covered over and protected by the body.

At this stage, the noises might bear little relationship to the movement sequence, and this would be developed later when the handling is really familiar.

(c) Playing the instrument with different sound qualities and relating the movement to it; *e.g.*, play lightly and gently on, say, a gong which swings easily as the moving person sways and swings lightly from side to side; turning and travelling, *e.g.*, play with vigour and strength on, say, a tambourine, creating a violent rattling and banging which is accompanied by vigorous jumps and stamps and shakes; play with lightness, increasing strength, a gradual crescendo or, vice versa, in a crescendo (*see* Chapter 3), when the movement works up to a climax stopping at the peak, or down to a quietness and pause. Rhythmical variations can be encouraged and developed according to the skill and knowledge of the class.

As well as always moving exactly with the sound, it is possible to create counter-effects by moving without playing and, on the pause and stillness in movement, letting the sound take over, a kind of dramatic play between the sounds and the **moving**.

(*d*) Using the instrument as an opposing force or object to be reckoned with and reacted to: jumping over it, getting away from it, advancing towards it and picking it up, etc.

Working with a partner

(*a*) Each partner has an instrument to create a spontaneous "conversation" in movement and sound. Two dissimilar instruments make contrast and variation easy; two more-similar instruments can be used to stimulate ideas for their varied use. At the beginning, it is simpler to suggest "when one person moves and plays, the other holds a position," like a real conversation.

(*b*) "Talking together" is more difficult, but gradually a sensitivity of the relationships between the sounds (as well as the action) can be developed. These sequences should be kept short at first and repeated often.

(*c*) Using one instrument between two people (some instruments are in two parts: two cymbals, drum and beater, gong and beater, etc., and the hand can also be used as a beater), which stimulates the interplay between the two people. The necessity to synchronise the flow of movement between the partners becomes obvious, otherwise no contact is made.

Using percussion instruments

Working in a group

(*a*) One person has the instrument; the rest of the group take on the "character" of the instrument.

(*b*) All have a similar instrument and play and dance in unison.

Using percussion helps to develop the sensitivity of a class to quality, variations of accents and stresses, to rhythmical variations, free and regular, and it helps them to relate sound and movement in a natural way. Music usually gives a quite different experience, for there is very little melody and shape variation in percussion work. Mention should be made here of percussive sounds used as background noises when the sound sets a mood and atmosphere.

Many instruments are expensive, but there are endless possibilities of improvising and making your own. Drums, clappers, rattles and shakers can all be made of filled tins, pieces of wood, etc., even by young children. Gongs are expensive but sometimes cheap metal cases and blocks can be found which give a similar long sounding noise, when struck with a beater.

Example of a whole dance play incorporating the use of percussion (for young children)

A group of children surround a central pile of instruments, a strange shape in the centre of the group. They should imagine they have never seen any before. They advance towards them, some cautiously, some daringly, some excitedly, and one child dares to pick up an instrument and finds it makes a sound (watched by the others). They gradually choose their own instruments and go off, playing individually or with a partner. An outside sound (rumbling gong, drum, sharp clicking or voice melody) makes them cautious and apprehensive, and the return of the "magician of sound" makes them replace the instruments carefully and run off.

Many variations can be brought in : one child could keep his instrument and get caught, or the magician (as a person) could invite them back, or there could be no real magician at all, and so on.

CHAPTER 10

Action images taken from nature

I

MANY teachers find a stimulus for movement in the everyday happenings around them. Not only is this a natural stimulus, but a fundamental one, when we consider that movement study is concerned with the recognition of the patterns and rhythms of nature and the discovery of the fundamental movement laws of relationship which govern life.

In looking for movement happenings in nature, it is necessary to discriminate between the kind of imagery which evokes both a verbal or mental response (when a child would then paint, or write a poem or story), and a movement response (when a child then wants to dance or create a dramatic movement scene). Sometimes the same idea can evoke both of these different reactions, and it is the teacher's skill in presentation which will stimulate the kind of response desired. For instance, the idea of a volcano erupting can be a vivid movement stimulus. It could also be presented so that the pictorial aspect of the colour of smoke, flames, etc., is an overwhelming visual picture, which the child portrays either in words or with paints. It can also be described in such a way that the emotional reaction to the horror or splendour of the explosion and subsequent destruction is an experience for the hearers. Probably in this case there would be less stimulus to physical movement than to describe the emotions in words. This latter emotional reaction of changing moods, and feelings, may,

Action images taken from nature

however, serve as a stimulus for dramatic movement sequences or a dance form for older and more experienced groups. This goes beyond the immediate and simple stimulus of a natural happening, and deals with human feelings either typifying a general mood through the portrayal of a particular dramatic situation with individual characters, their actions and responses, or experiencing of the general mood (or moods) through a formulated dance, with carefully chosen movements within the range of this mood (very like a musical composition or tone poem).

Going back to the simple idea of the stimulus, if we take the movement content of our chosen natural happening and try to bring to our notice the many aspects of movement which are contained in the description, as well as in the coaching of the movement response, then the image can help the movement and not cause a distraction.

As an example, some of the movement ideas which lend themselves to an analogy with a volcanic eruption are set out in the table on page 76. Such an idea might be used for young children of junior age as sufficient movement play in itself. It might also be used as part of a longer sequence for more experienced children. The idea of converging, gathering and increasing strength followed by exploding out and away from a group might occur as a motive in a group dance, without any specific reference to a volcano.

Note the contrasting ideas of:

converging group and dispersing group
increasing tension and release
use of small amount of space and spreading in space
group and individual.

The phrasing and rhythmical development should also be considered. This will arise naturally from the group movement and, if many groups work at the same time, many variations of timing will be recognised. As the sequence is repeated, the movement happenings should become more exact, the rhythmic phrases better known and repeated, and definite starting positions

Idea chosen from nature: a volcanic eruption

In the action three parts can be discerned (See Chapter 4)	Body	Accents and rhythm	Space directions	Relationship
1. Preparation	Movement arising or converging towards the centre of the body. Extremities of the body concentrating and narrowing inwards. See Chapters 1 and 2	Gathering of strength towards a peak, i.e., variations, e.g., (a) slow concentrating and increasing strength (b) rhythmically phrased, increasing in speed and strength. See Chapter 3	Converging to a single centre (spoke-like movement). Probably also lifting from low to high. See Chapter 2	Could be alone, but probably better as a group movement. Converging group towards single central focus, gradually increasing contact and pressure; easier at first with three or five in group. See Chapters 2 and 11
2. Explosion	Dispersal from the centre into the extremities. See Chapters 1 and 2	Sudden bursting out, with dispersal and decrease of energy. See Chapter 3	Dispersing in all directions away from the centre. Can also be taken literally into a high explosion. See Chapter 2	Scatter away from each other about the room, taking on chosen part (a), (b) or (c) below. See Chapter 11
3. Result variable according to choice, e.g., (a) like the molten lava (b) like pieces of broken rock (c) Like smoke	(a) Changing, formless shapes (b) Retaining shape, perhaps jagged and rolling away from place of explosion (c) Bodily twisting and curling, counter-movements of different parts of the body. See Chapters 5 and 6	(a) Continuous flow and continuity and ominous, sustained pressure, with power (b) Held strong position, retaining hardness as shape rolls (c) Twisting and curling ebb and flow of light and strong, gradually decreasing and dispersing. See Chapters 3 and 5	(a) travelling horizontally or sinking down, curved pathways (b) Travelling along the floor low, occasionally bouncing or leaping, then settling down, holding shape at the end (c) Interweaving pathways up and down. See Chapter 5	(a) Joining two or more together to make mass (b) Single pieces (c) Individuals within group twisting and curling (also with locomotion).

Action images taken from nature

and ending positions chosen. A growing awareness of phrasing can be encouraged by the accompanying of the movement by sounds made by the children as they move. These sounds should have the same increase and decrease, crescendo and decrescendo as the movement.

In presenting ideas to the class, the teacher must decide which aspects of movement are to be stressed first, and which are at that moment secondary, *e.g.*, in a lesson where the emphasis is on working together, the space and direction aspects might well be allowed to stay in the background. In a lesson where the interest is mainly on encouraging the composition of free rhythmical phrases, less emphasis might be laid on large group relationships.

The example quoted above is essentially a sequence of happenings (where the main movement idea is concerned with accent, stress and free rhythmical sequence, *see* Chapters 3 and 4). There are many other "forces" in nature which give a stimulus to movement, some as sequences with contrasts, others retaining a single "force." Such forces include magnetism, whirling, suction, crystallising, melting and precipitation. It is useful to take these and find another example (which might also be taken from a poem or passage which describes the natural force) and clarify the different aspects of movement contained within it for yourself in a way similar to the above example. In presentation to the class, you might never mention the stimulus, but, by becoming aware of the many-sidedness of a movement happening, your observation of the class will be directed, and it will help you in giving constructive criticism.

II

When using an image to stimulate movement and dance, there are two main methods of presentation to the class:

1. The idea – poem, description or even single word – can be

Introduction to movement study and teaching

given to the class (with as little or as much emphasis and inspiration as the teacher desires) and the class or individual reaction can be observed and helped. This method leaves the choice and particular movement ideas to the class, and the teacher must be prepared to accept ideas other than those which might have been personally envisaged.

The idea can stimulate the teacher to compose a movement or dance sequence which is presented to the class. If the children are to make the main part of the composition themselves, the spontaneous response of the class is noted after the initial stimulus is given, and it is the teacher's task to help the development of these movement ideas. There is occasionally a place for the spontaneous response of the class being accepted, and no further work on it being done. But in general, over the years, an increasing participation and experience can be gained by a class if spontaneous movement happenings are helped to grow and develop beyond the initial attempt. The older the children, the less satisfied will they be to make continuously improvised reactions which are never developed further. The teacher faces a difficult task in trying to observe which are the important movement ideas which the child or group chooses. Frequently, these are unconscious and unrecognised by the moving persons themselves, and have arisen from the "feel of the movement." To make conscious and to clarify these fundamental ideas, without imposing the teacher's own interpretation, or suppressing growing movement ideas, is a skill which can be developed:

(*a*) By clear observation, so that the intention, however hidden or blurred, can be seen.

(*b*) By knowledge of the movement possibilities, so that guidance towards clarity and choice of movement can be given, as described in part I of this chapter.

(*c*) By understanding the needs and abilities of the particular class, so that the sequence, dance or drama is developed within the range of the group, being neither too easily achieved, nor too advanced for satisfaction to be gained.

Action images taken from nature

Unless the class is very experienced, it will be necessary not only to stimulate the idea or mood in general, but to provide a concrete situation from which the movement can develop. For instance, taking the example used in part I, the class should be challenged: "Where will you begin? Choose your starting place. As you move, you want to become tighter or narrower and closer together. Where would it be helpful to start? In your starting place, be ready for your first movement. Which part of you is going to move first? Where will it move? Then prepare for it . . ."

Such preparation is necessary as an inner focusing of attention to the coming movement, whatever it is to be. The starting situation can then be repeated and gives a security for the subsequent movement happenings. Children will understand this as being like a capital letter at the beginning of a sentence. Equally, a full stop at the end indicates that the sentence is finished. So, with a movement or dance sequence, the ending situation should be held, quite still, for a moment. The position and shape should be clear. Ask: "Are you near the ground or high up? Away from others or close together? Twisted and screwed round or open wide . . . ?" The meaning should be clearly seen. Ask: "Are you strong and solid (like a rock) or weak and collapsing, or very light and airy . . . ?" and so on. Both the beginning and ending situations can be "surprise" situations (*i.e.*, unexpected from what follows or precedes the position) but, in general, and particularly at first, it is easier to relate the starting situation to an easily recognised following movement and to ensure that, in the ending, the previous movement should be recognised (like the stopping of the movement, *see* Chapter 5). Contrasts, unexpected and grotesque variations are all part of movement play, but probably the simple straightforward beginnings and endings should first be mastered. (These comments on the necessity to encourage beginning and end situations are, of course, relevant to the whole of the movement and dance teaching and not only to this section.)

In taking as a stimulus trees, flowers, etc., there is the danger of presenting or selecting those aspects of movement which are less important so that the real idea is lost. No one can "be" a tree or flower and only to a certain extent can he represent a living thing from his own experience. What is possible is for someone to move like, or to be inspired to move by, the chosen object; to experience, in fact, the movement qualities and patterns which are there. Growing and shrinking are such familiar movement happenings, experienced in our own lives, and observed continuously in all living things. It is therefore not surprising that the theme has an immediate response. If we do not limit the conception of growing to a particular thing, the variety of response is infinite, for the combinations of movement and their development have no limit. Some of the main groupings of movement ideas can be observed in the following:

(*a*) Growing in size: a small thing becomes a large thing; from being closed and small it extends into space.

(*b*) Growing in a definite direction, usually upwards, but also horizontally (like roots); changing directions, making a twisted way or jagged path.

(*c*) Growing in intensity and strength.

(*d*) Growing in speed and urgency.

(*e*) Repetition of a rhythmical phrase, growing in intensity and/or urgency.

(*f*) Increasing number of people joining a group.

Examples of "growing" are described here as observed in three different children in a six-year-old class:

Child A starts with a curved body shape – lightly forward – and lifts his head as the first movement. He grows in size, from low to high. There is light, swaying movement with a quality of sensitivity and ease. The pathway is a series of curves, starting small, becoming larger, ultimately leading the child away from the spot. The ending is spread wide and flowing. This was a spontaneous sequence, but was repeated fairly exactly immediately after.

Child B starts with his body shape small and round. The fingers first begin to spike out, "like a cactus" (which they have in the school hall). There is a slight upward growing,

Action images taken from nature

mainly around the body in all directions, spiking out. There are increasingly frequent and strong jerky movements as the body grows bigger. At the end of the sequence, the child holds the spiky shape.

Child C starts strongly twisted but upright, near the ground, growing up in a twisted way. The child said it was "very hard to grow." Ultimately he rises higher but never extends. At the climax there is a momentary hold, and a sudden collapse to the ground at the end.

These were all self-chosen ways stimulated by the idea of "growing" presented by the teacher.

2. The second way in which an idea can be used is when the teacher is stimulated to compose a movement or dance sequence which is presented to the class. In this case, it should be given genuinely as a definite idea, to be followed by the class, and the aim is then a common movement experience, not a spontaneous individual response.

The teacher or leader makes the selection from the wide range of possibilities, and composes them into a sequence or dance. Such ideas might include ebb and flow, opening and closing, rising and falling, advancing and retiring, meeting and parting, converging and dispersing, whirling and stopping, flying and falling.

It is useful to take combinations of these or similar ideas and build a sequence of happenings, using definite and clear situations.

CHAPTER 11

Group movement: relationships with others

A SPECIAL chapter on group work is included because this is perhaps one of the outstanding features of dance and movement as an educational means. It is unnecessary to state the obvious resulting values of tolerance, understanding and co-operation which participation in well-developed group movement and dance compositions can provide. The development of a sense of values in working with others in all present-day relationships can only be a positive contribution to society and the individual.

It is my opinion that, in however simple a form, group action in dancing or dramatic situations should be started straightaway with a class and developed parallel with the growing experience of individual movement. Perhaps the only exception to this would be in a very young class of infants but, even there, I think there is a place for occasionally experiencing unison movement with all the children doing the same, perhaps rhythmically held together, or even a movement stimulus based on a relationship there as simple as weaving in and out of each other or diving under or over someone else. The focus is entirely different from exclusive absorption on one's own individual movement, although, naturally, this personal exploration will form the largest part of the lesson for the very young. Individual work, partner work and group work should all be developed simultaneously over the years.

All the movement ideas which have been dealt with in the earlier chapters can be used either individually or in relation to others, *e.g.*

Group movement: relationships with others

Chapter 1. A group can be symmetrically balanced or asymmetrically formed, and can alternate between the two.

Chapter 2. The "group body" can contract into a small space and expand and spread out, each person (like each limb or body part of the individual) getting closer to – even touching – or getting further from everyone else.

Chapter 3. The group can have a central focus and individuals move together in and out towards the centre (which may be a person, an inner group, or a space). The resulting circular and star patterns are familiar in most country dances, ritual dance forms and social dancing.

Chapter 4. Unison rising and falling of a group into the space above and below, or the travelling of the group body, advancing, retiring or sideways moving. Counter-directional movements (*e.g.*, one group surrounded by another, the one rising as the other sinks) make for lively contrast and emphasise one experience compared with another.

Just as one part of the body may move in a counter-direction to another (*e.g.*, walking forward, with a backward leaning of the body, feet or knees going first, and a tilting of the head to one side) so a group can within itself create counter-tensions. An obvious example is of, say, a large group representing a ship battling through heavy oceans: the front tilts down, the rear lifts, the one side crumples in, the other tilts over, while the next movement reverses this, and gives the rocking, rolling, lurching of a ship at sea. There is a great degree of co-operation and subtle adjusting for each child as a member of the group to achieve the gradual changes always in relation to each other as part of the group. The responsibility to "pass on" the movement both by touch and sight is important and one unco-operative member can ruin the experience.

The group phrases its actions and movements, needing preparations and recoveries in the same way as an individual. Phrasing is almost always longer in group action than individual work (*e.g.*, it takes longer for a group to turn on its axis than an individual) and it frequently takes longer to take over

Introduction to movement study and teaching

a new movement as it has to be "passed along" to others.

Chapter 5. Mention has already been made of group shapes comparable with individual shapes.

Chapter 7. Air and floor patterns resulting from group movement will be differently balanced, needing more space and frequently making different angles in order to manoeuvre the less manageable body.

Apart from these aspects of movement which relate to group and partner work, there are certain themes which are inherently relationship ideas and cannot be performed by one person alone (except sometimes with an imaginary partner or group). A few examples are breaking through and splitting a group (minimum three persons), capturing and surrounding (minimum two individuals or groups, but preferably more), passing along a movement shape or rhythm (minimum two individuals or groups, but preferably more), and meeting and parting (minimum two persons).

SOME IDEAS FOR PARTNER RELATIONSHIP WORK (OR TWO GROUPS)

Basically there are four possibilities:

    meeting
    leaving or parting
    passing by
    staying with.

All can be performed at varied levels with different rhythms, accents, phrases, expressions. The four possibilities appear in any sequence of happenings, *e.g.*

    1. Exploring the idea of magnetism as a force between two bodies. This may result in a sequence between A (the active force, like a magnet) and B (the non-active, like a pin).

A approaches B, leads B on a journey: B must follow (added interest arises when a specific part of the body is "magnetised," *e.g.*, fingers, knee, shoulder, and A chooses with which part B shall be obliged to follow). Imaginative leading and accurate

Group movement: relationships with others

following can result in amusing and challenging situations. An ending could be designed for the finish of the sequence, for instance B might acquire the strength to resist and after a struggle break away, leaving A weak and powerless, collapsing, while B is free and active. Obviously, the whole story could be repeated in reverse, B leading A. The idea of one person following the lead of another can be thus developed with an action story to help.

2. Following the lead of a partner can be developed in a dance-like way, in rhythmical phrases which can be repeated, and gradually the motifs will become known and the two people will move together in unison. This can be very symmetric, like the mirroring of action, or asymmetric, where different parts of the body are used and only the shape and phrasing are in unison.

The obvious training resulting from this experience of leading and following is (for the follower) co-operation, quick adaptability and anticipation; (for the leader) sensitivity, clarity and concern for the follower. A clear indication of each preparation for action is important, and it will be found necessary for the leader to repeat the same phrase and rhythm a few times if any attempt is made to lead other than in a slow, shaped and controlled way.

3. Passing a movement from one to the other – *e.g.*, a shape which is followed through, a rhythm which is continued or a phrase which is ended. Succession of movement from one body part or person to another requires similar clarity, awareness and anticipation (in order not to "drop the ball").

4. Question and answer in movement conversation, *i.e.*, alternating movement; while one is still, holding his position, the other moves. Conversation challenge can be:

(*a*) In body position or attitude, *e.g.*,

A leaps high and poises looking down on B;
B responds by shrinking down to the ground;

Introduction to movement study and teaching

A follows by pressing down to medium level;
B reacts by twisting away, getting free and challenging A from a distance, broad, firm and strong;
A weakens pressure and turns away and so on . . .

(*b*) In rhythmical phrasing into these positions, *e.g.*,
A bouncy;
B slow and pedantic;
A light and tentative and so on . . .

(*c*) In drawing complementary shapes, air and floor patterns.

Gradually the couple can select and fix a sequence of actions and reactions to complete a whole "movement story": a starting situation, a sequence of actions and an ending situation. To help beginners, it may be necessary to give directions for timing, *e.g.*, A moves (wait until all A's have finished), now B moves, and so on, but the teacher will not need to do that often, unless there is a particular discipline problem to be faced.

5. One partner (or group) acts as an obstacle, providing spaces, gaps and a definite shape for the other to go through, round, over or under. While the partner is perfectly still, this is a simple working with an obstacle. As an advanced challenge, the obstacle can slowly change shape and the second person should try to achieve his object by speedy and accurate adjustments. It is sometimes necessary to make the challenge to avoid touching the obstacle.

6. Working together with a partner to become one body, *e.g.*, to progress down the room. Young boys seem to enjoy being bound together like a ball, and rolling, wheelbarrow combinations, continuous somersaulting while each child holds his partner's ankles, three-legged adjustments, etc., also prove popular.

Restricting the movement by specific challenges which have to be fulfilled and adding the requirement of selection from improvisations to build a sequence or dance gives working scope

Group movement: relationships with others

for invention, at a play level for youngsters, or in a dance or drama form for older children.

Group work has many aspects and each can contribute to the developing awareness of the children. A certain progression can be seen, though not necessarily in this strict order. Without doubt, some group actions are easier than others.

(a) The simplest form is probably when everyone does the same movement at the same time: even the youngest children can experience the difference between converging on a spot (perhaps with the teacher in the centre) and feeling close and secure as a group and the gradual loosening of the group until each one has room to move alone. Incidentally, the conception of "find your own space," though admirable for performing personal movement, can be mistakenly used with very young and timid children, who cluster together for security when confronted with a large space. This can be used as a game – to come close and gradually spread, only to return close – and the children will soon feel the need for space when absorbed in larger personal action. Unison movement, like growing up, surrounding the centre, covering it over, etc., has a definite place from the very beginning.

(b) It is advisable for a leader to be chosen whose movements the group has to follow. There is at the beginning no sense of group sensitivity other than an awareness that "we all do the same thing." This task (and I suggest it should not be presented in too large a group, say in fives or sevens) stimulates observation by the followers and clear, decisive action, and waiting for the group, by the leader. At the beginning, it is necessary to give the children specific movement ideas and challenges for leading their group, *e.g.*, taking the group from one place to another with rising and sinking actions, such as swooping and diving (leaving the rhythm and phrasing to the leader's choice).

The leader cannot do as he likes; he must be aware of the large body behind him and be sensitive to its needs. In manoeuvring the group, adjustments might have to be made

Introduction to movement study and teaching

by different group members but, primarily, all will be performing the same movement. The leader must not change his movement too quickly; he must wait for the group and it helps if the movement is repeated and phrased. His movement must be large enough to be seen (*i.e.*, go very high and deep down). Any movement occurring in front of the leader must be shown by:

(*i*) leading from a bigger to smaller movement or
(*ii*) starting the movement far away and bringing it closer.

The followers must react quickly and, if in a big group, take the movement from the person in front as the leader may not be seen. They must learn to respond and adapt to the quality as well as the shape of the movement and keep their relative position in the group. At this level, the movement is still the main consideration and the relationships secondary. In encouraging group awareness, the relationships become primary and the movement secondary. Ultimately, of course, both are united.

(*c*) Belonging together in a group will probably first be experienced through touch: an easy development comes via partner work, with one partner leading the other through touching (this can be tried with the follower's eyes closed). Small groups of three or more together can touch and try to respond to the give and take as it arises in common sinking, rising, turning and precipitating movements. One central person can act as a body with others as extensions to right and left, holding hands, and becoming like the wings of a bird, swooping, winding up, like trailing "arms," tilting one side high and one low, and so on, with a definite lead coming from the central person.

It is an interesting theme for movement play, as well as dance and drama composition, to contrast the freedom of individual movement and action with the unison group action, which limits personal freedom, and demands both discipline and responsibility.

In group work, we are concerned with common purpose, action and focus. Sometimes the leader arises from the group and sometimes he is a person outside the action like a conductor, who can control the person or group with direction, such as "come here," "bend up close," "sink down," etc. A conductor with two people, one for each hand, has a more difficult task to control and correlate the two actions, not only giving pathways and directions, but rhythms and qualities. Two groups can be substituted for the two people and the situation becomes like the conductor of a moving orchestra or choir.

DANCE AND DRAMA

It is clear that both partner and group work (and individual too) can develop either into dance or dramatic action. All of the ideas suggested are for movement exploration or play. They are, however, the basis of movement ideas used in composing dances and dance dramas or mimes. In my opinion, the work in secondary schools should be at the level of composed dances or dramas and not restricted to (and often not even approached via) movement exploration. The artistic activity of composing dances cannot be learned by reading a book and although there are fundamental principles of composition, they are the same as those inherent in any creative artistic activity: conception of the whole, followed by selection of the material suitable to support the conception. The act of creating a dance is a personal one; it can be conceived and then developed or it can grow from improvisation which is refined and composed. It is sufficient to state that, given the opportunity and guidance where needed, children will compose as delightful "works of art" as they will paint pictures and compose poems.

Perhaps it might be useful to make a general statement about the difference between a composition in drama, dramatic play or dance drama and a dance composition. Drama deals with situations between people or groups of people (whether specifically characterised, or of general "type"). The development of the composition is based on the sequence of action, reaction and further action, from one situation to the next. Dance deals with universal patterns and rhythms and has a logic and development, not of situation to situation, but of motif and forms, growing and shrinking, increasing and decreasing, like music. If drama gives a picture of the universal in a particular situation, dance "tunes in" to the rhythm and pattern of the universe itself.

It will be expected that the patterns and formations which occur in group work will have special significance in composition.

(*a*) The parallelism and symmetry of equal groups and lines, *i.e.*, lack of tension.

(*b*) The position of groups or lines in creating tension and conflict.

(*c*) The curving, adaptable, waving line.

(*d*) The unity of a circular pattern, where all are equal, or the revolving, like a wheel.

(*e*) The concentration of a spiralling.

(*f*) The twisting and counter-tension of a figure-of-eight.

(*g*) The rigidity of line and block, even and mechanical, like soldiers.

(*h*) The changing shapes of arrows, walls, balls and twists, where each person becomes only a part of a group shape (as discussed previously in Chapter 5).

In dance, the formations and patterns change and develop within themselves or in contrast to other patterns. In drama and dance drama, these formations may change violently or gradually in adapting to a situation of conflict, *e.g.*, a wedge breaking through a line and spinning off the pieces, an assembly of scattered individuals to make a group or profession, etc.

Taking part in movement compositions where formation and pattern play a large part gives the children a strong sense of discipline and regard for others in a common endeavour; not a discipline from outside, but a self-discipline to support and contribute to the composition.

COMPOSITION

Composition of group movement can be learned by the teacher

Group movement: relationships with others

and the children through practice and an awareness of elementary principles.

The overall meaning must be decided upon, either as the first step, or during the development of the composition. The style should be constant throughout the composition, *e.g.*, *lyrical* (where the pure movement phrases, patterns and shapes are stressed); *ritual* (where the idea is developed in stylised movement and groups, and frequently taken from a particular geographical area, group or tribe); *grotesque* (where contrast of movement, distortion or body shape and, often, rhythm and the unexpected action predominates); *mimetic* (where caricature and individual mime play is chosen – very frequently this can start from children's observations of body shapes and typical rhythmical actions); *dramatic group action* and interaction (either of characters or of "types" (sailors, clowns, etc.)).

The more lyrical or formal the composition, the greater use will be made of repetition of motifs, development of motifs and phrases, and variations in space, shape and rhythm. Even mime is similarly repetitive when the style is nearer to "dance mime" than to straight mime.

Dramatic movement ranges from the literal portrayal of dramatic action, to the rhythmicised, repeated actions of the participants, *i.e.*, from "straight drama" to "dance drama."

The composition should develop organically from the necessity to express the meaning, *i.e.*, it is quite different from having a series of movement patterns, arranged and ordered. The choice of *motifs* arises from the requirement of the theme; the composition lasts as long as the theme requires to be expanded. This is not the same as making an "exercise" sequence on a particular movement idea, *e.g.*, turning, or opening and closing, which may be well composed, but is still a study.

Music may be used as a starting point, either to be followed formally and exactly, or as a background phrasing. When music is chosen, it should be a simple, complete piece, and should be followed exactly. Here the form and discipline are provided by the music and the movement must weave into its fabric. Fre-

Introduction to movement study and teaching

quently, it is preferable to work from the movement, developing the "movement logic," and fixing the rhythmical phrases and patterns, probably in a freer style (though not every time different). This can be in silence, or can be a stimulus for voice or percussion accompaniment.

The main or first aim of the teacher should not be to produce a composition to be looked at, but to work from "inside," and it will be evident that, if this is appropriately developed, it also looks interesting for spectators. The danger in producing, or choreographing, from "outside," to look good, is that the movement becomes contrived and artificial.

CHAPTER 12

Movement, colour and pattern

THIS chapter comprises comments on some of the ways in which movement and the visual arts relate. The experiments have been conducted over many years with children, students and adult recreative groups. The children have enjoyed the work and have been stimulated to produce paintings, masks, costumes, percussion instruments, mobiles, models and sculptures. Students and adults who have "never done any painting" have been led gradually to experiment with colour and materials and to overcome initial reluctance and shyness. As often happens, many people who have no background training in "art" have spontaneously produced satisfying pictures and models with an unspoiled simplicity and natural flair for composition.

The aims in working with these varied groups have been different according to age and experience. For adults the aim is to re-awaken the lost spontaneity in producing paintings and models, to overcome the fear of handling the materials, to learn to see – and not only look for – colours and shapes, as they use them, choose them and make special selections from the wide range of possibilities, and thereby to become more appreciative of colour and design in everyday life. This applies in decorating their own houses, in choosing furniture and china, pictures and clothes. We aimed to draw their attention to the influence of colour on a person's reactions, his likes and dislikes (which can change) and to the appropriateness of colour to situations and materials; to help them to appreciate the calmness of some colour combinations, and the difference between the calm and the restlessness of exciting textures; to encourage them to experiment with the contrast between clear and textured surfaces or hot and cool colours; to show them how the size of a room or a piece of paper and relative positions can influence the effect of the whole, and to recognise that the restrained use of contrast can highlight the impact of a colour or shape. They came to see that some arrangements and colours are fussy and agitated, others severe and so on. I believe that there is a direct carry-over into everyday situations of this recognition of colour and form. It is obviously helped enormously if the teacher or leader can direct awareness into these channels by drawing examples, parallels and illustrations, *e.g.*, by reference to the room they work in, their clothes and the objects in the room or sometimes by showing pictures. Teachers should always be ready to pick up and exploit a situation.

There are so many obvious parallels between aspects of movement and visual pattern, form and colour. This chapter assumes that the teacher who has reached this stage of study in movement will be able to see these inter-relationships; *i.e.*, that body shapes in space are like block shapes in two- or three-dimensional visual art, that pathways – both air patterns and floor patterns – relate to lines along which the eye can move, just as the body itself draws patterns in space, that colour, texture and light and shade are like effort qualities and moods of movement – vigorous, peaceful, agitated, etc. – and are enhanced by their being juxtaposed. A too literal drawing of equivalents between visual rhythms, shapes and colours and movement qualities, shapes and forms becomes both tedious and banal, but my experience is that sensibility in one area tends to enhance responsiveness in the other.

EXAMPLE OF A CHALLENGE GIVEN TO AN ADULT BEGINNER GROUP

Each member of the group was asked to make an arrangement of objects: living material (plants, leaves, etc.) or natural objects (stones, bark) or manufactured objects and materials (boxes, paper, balls, etc.). Given the idea to collect objects – starting with any one – the students chose the next to go with it, each doing so in a personal way. They chose mainly from the viewpoints of:

> Colour, texture and "feel" of the objects.
> Shapes and sizes.
> Idea associations (*e.g.*, one young woman started with an old root of a bush lying above ground and chose bark, fungus, leaves and berries, and arranged them to indicate "dead things changing into live fruitful growth").
> Objects linked independently in themselves.

Having collected the objects, the group was asked to arrange them attractively, in a place of their own choosing, indoors or outdoors.

The arrangements varied from the tasteful and selective to a crude and unselective piling together. Each arrangement was looked at and discussed from the point of view of both choice and arrangement. Examples are quoted below from a small and limited range of the work of the group when a specific restriction of living things – branches, leaves, flowers – was given, with the intention of giving some experience and awareness in flower arrangement.

The arrangements were placed:

> Flat on the floor or on a piece of paper, like a two-dimensional drawing, *i.e.*, viewed from above.
> In a corner, which enclosed the arrangement on three sides and gave a framework, *i.e.*, restricted front view.
> In a vase, *i.e.*, supported from below and allowing an all-round view from every side.
> Against a wall or window as background, *i.e.*, a wider front view, or even "seeing through" with light behind.
> Suspended from a height, *i.e.*, view from below.

The choice of arranging indoors or outdoors gave a different character to the grouping: outside dictated a "natural" arrangement, while the indoor work included natural arrangements, but

Introduction to movement study and teaching

also more abstract designs, patterns and "idea" arrangements.

This led to discussion of the appropriateness of certain arrangements to situations, the limitations and the freedoms within these "frameworks." The arrangements themselves were:

Natural (three-dimensional), as though growing from a central source, as a plant mainly grows from one area or point, in vases and as bouquets. This kind of arrangement was mostly limited to branches, flowers and live growing things and either symmetrical (*see* Chapter 1), balanced by equal things – in its simplest form, three things – or asymmetrical, balanced in a more mobile way by different things.

Circular and wheel formations (*see* Chapters 2 and 11), like a garland, one with the colours changing gradually round the circle; another a purely patterned idea and more repetitive; or a star shape, a pattern which follows the familiar formation of a single flower. Sometimes there were colour changes from the centre and outside. The arrangements were rarely haphazard in colour and shape.

Flat, line-like arrangements, mainly two-dimensional, but a few were not completely flat, with changes in colour or size.

Three-dimensional arrangements, material sticking into the ground, or some other object which was found, *e.g.*, wood, turf, bark.

The motifs were various:

Shapes – long pieces (branches, stems, etc.), rounded fruits, flowers, mushrooms, etc.

Colour changes – either contrasts or "near" colours.

Odd materials of general "mood," *e.g.*, old twisted wire, dead bark, soil, shrivelled leaves and fruits.

An idea – *e.g.*, autumn colours, fruits and richness giving way to dead things of winter, a hint of colour and new flowers for spring. Some were "airy," with the spaces which were left in between the arranged objects playing a significant part in the composition. Others were "solid" in building, *i.e.*, the materials usually resting one on another. Whole arrangements were sometimes of tiny things, *e.g.*, one leaf holding a multitude of detail: berries, nuts, etc.

When the materials chosen were manufactured or man-made objects (and sometimes they do mix with natural ones, and sometimes there is an incongruity if they are mixed), the arrangements were dictated by the greater rigidity of form. At this point, it was found helpful to look at examples of modern architecture – blocks of flats, schools, etc. – and to look at modern advertisements. Examples of good and weak design were spotted fairly easily. Design in teapots and china and pots, and in contemporary furniture, was of particular interest to one group. Another group digressed to finding out different styles and taste in previous epochs. Other ideas arose from visits to the Design Centre, from catalogues, and from trying out a shop window arrangement (*e.g.*, one shoe-shop window design was most successful, using simple material: a book, walking shoes and coloured papers and material, trying to bring the sensation of country to the shopper in town). Leaving lots of space gave an ease and simplicity which was most effective. Drawing the attention of the group by "have a look at . . . and describe it next week" awakens interest, and has proved a fruitful way to link the personal experiments to everyday life.

I believe it is easy to make false and far-fetched parallels if one tries to link visual art too exactly with movement ideas. After all, the one is seen and appreciated "all in one piece"; the other, movement, occurs in time, and develops over a period, as does music, with a beginning and ending movement. Nevertheless, there are general parallels, such as the following:

Symmetry or asymmetry of the movement or pattern (*see* Chapter 1), just as, in sound and music, there are even or uneven rhythms and phrases.

Solid stability and stillness or restless change (*see* Chapter 5). In painting and other visual arts, it is the eye which is led restlessly on, along broken lines, shooting from one object or

Introduction to movement study and teaching

shape to the next, as well as the violent contrasts of colours which give restlessness. In music, the continuous evenness and smoothness of long phrases, note values and the lack of sudden changes make for calmness – the opposite for restlessness.

Colours and qualities or moods of movement and colour can be compared as, in music, can different rhythms and accents.

Gradual changes from one colour to another. As in movement there are transitions from one quality to another, so in music, one may find smooth changes of key and transitions.

Rough and smooth textures like jerky and smooth movement or, in music, staccato and legato playing.

Fine, delicate line and colour and pattern, like much of Chinese and Japanese art, correspond with lightness and sensitivity in movement and pianissimo in music. Bold, strong colours, bulk and line are like firm, forceful movement and, in music, forte playing (*see* Chapter 3).

Shape patterns on paper or in material have an exact parallel with drawing air patterns and floor patterns with the body as one dances through space, like a melody in music (*see* Chapter 8).

Block shapes are like body shapes or like a chord in music (*see* Chapter 5). Sometimes there is a direct link, in that the necessary movement to produce a visual effect is exactly parallel, *e.g.*, to draw a fine, delicate line, a light sensitive touch is essential, while a thick, bold line needs more "gripped" movement (but such parallels are not necessarily so – a thick brush and lots of paint may still result in a heavy line, even if a fine touch is used). The flow and continuity of a line is best achieved by a flowing movement while insecure movement often results in stilted lines and rough edges, like a child gripping too hard on a brush or pencil in an attempt to "keep on the line."

Symbolic shapes appear in both movement and visual art forms – circles, crosses, stars, etc. In movement, the symbolic shape may be as the body holds a position, *e.g.*, standing upright with arms outstretched in wonder or kneeling or bow-

Movement, colour and pattern

ing down in submission or spreading horizontal, arm outward and forward in blessing. The symbolic shape may be a transient one, drawn as a gesture is made, *e.g.*, moving over high, and opening out – a gesture of, perhaps, wonder or awe.

In early arrangements, there sometimes will appear an attempt to say in visual form what might be more appropriate in, for instance, words or sound, *e.g.*, the use of a drawn line, denoting passage in time, or sequence of events (as changes from autumn to winter to spring). Perhaps the real visual form of this would be contained in the design not depending upon a sequence travelling along a line (like an exhibition description) but the conception of winter and spring being forever inherent in autumn.

STIMULATING CREATIVE WORK WITH COLOUR

Very simple equipment – large paper, brushes large and small, and powder paints – have always proved adequate for this exploratory stage.

First, the student should make himself familiar with the material: holding and handling the brush, and finding out how to mix the paint. This often needs patient and slow leading of a group, particularly when the group is mainly composed of restrained and lethargic adults; sometimes it is even necessary to be as simple as: "Try out your brush on the paper dry, just to feel it. Sweep over the paper. Gently touch the paper. Press on to it. Dab it lightly. Make short jerky strokes and then twisted, whirling ones. Now wet the brush, and take some powder which sticks to it – choose which colour you like (primary colours, plus black and white) and mix on a plate."

Challenge 1

The students could start by putting a patch of the colour they have chosen on to the paper. For the hesitant ones (and they may be the majority in a beginner group of adults while children will normally be less inhibited) it could be suggested that the patch might be a tiny dot, a big splodge, a wriggly line, a square or a rough area. Then they should choose another to put next to it, and gradually cover the page, always looking at what is produced and deciding which colour to use next and where to put it. (At first, there should be no limitation to the number of colours used, no suggestion of mixing or how to apply.) It is interesting to put the resulting pictures together at the end (the impact of the lively colour is always stimulating for the group to see) and to comment to the whole group briefly about the differences and similarities; often at first the designs are mainly squiggles on a page, with lots of background of paper showing; sometimes there is intuitively an arrangement of the colours, sometimes very little.

Colour combinations chosen show many variations:

(*a*) Every colour available haphazardly placed.
(*b*) Many colours carefully arranged and balanced.
(*c*) Limited choice of colours in range and number; particularly this might happen if previous work with objects had been commented on from a colour point of view.
(*d*) Weak, pale colours.
(*e*) Solid strong colours. (Sometimes (*d*) and (*e*) are combined.)

Comments from the group usually arise from:

Noticing the wide area of background left so that the colours were all affected by white (or background colour).

Noticing that some were line arrangements rather than colour contrasts.

Noticing any variations (*e.g.*, occasionally someone will merge the colours, making a general wettish effect).

Noticing the block colours in some; this gives rise to the idea of how different a colour can look according to what it is near, *e.g.*, the same yellow looks brighter if next to black, greener if next to blue, pinker if next to red and so on (this often leads to discussion of wall colours in decorating a room).

The obvious developments of this challenge are to be more specific, *e.g.*

(*a*) That the colours should actually touch each other with no background showing. If it shows, it is deliberately left as a colour.

(b) Careful choice of colours.

(c) Perhaps to separate colours by another colour in maybe a line, linking two or three of them.

(d) Pale or strong colours by choice.

Obviously all these challenges cannot be coped with at once by everyone; the teacher must discriminate the speed and development with each particular group.

I give a few more examples in less detail of possible challenges with some of the results which have been achieved.

Challenge 2

Choosing colours which are "nextdoor neighbours" to put beside each other, so there is no shock in the change and no quick contrast. The resulting choices were:

(a) Hard, clear colours, near in intensity.

(b) Watery, pale colours, near through watering down to pastel shades.

(c) Near through whitening every colour.

(d) Near through blackening colours.

(e) Near through nearness of colours themselves, e.g., yellow/orange/red range or blue/purple/mauve range.

In setting the task for the first time, I had expected result (e) but the other variations equally fulfilled the task. (In movement, this is like using effort actions of a nearby nature, e.g., press/thrust/dab), or increasing or decreasing gradually in intensity in a phrase (*see* Chapter 3).)

Challenge 3

Choosing colours which are contrasting. In all cases, strong, vital colours resulted, though one could imagine also contrasts of weak and strong in the same picture.

Challenge 4

Merging colours, *i.e.*, mixing colours so that no clear edge is apparent.

Challenge 5

Blocking colours, with clear edges, and shapes therefore arising.

Challenge 6

Experimenting with the influence of one colour on another. Mixing colours in the palette, encouraging richness of choice.

(*a*) Put one colour on the paper, add one new colour to it, then another, seeing how one colour changes another.

(*b*) Start with one colour, adding increasing quantities of one other colour.

(*c*) Use only one colour, in increasing strength (or weakness).

Merging colours on the paper.

(*a*) Wet merging, running colours into one another.

(*b*) Dry merging when colours are deliberately painted to overlap.

(*c*) Use one basic colour, over which other colours are painted to give a hazy effect or a change of colour. Textures can be changed by placement of new colours (dots, shadings, crisscrosses, etc.).

(*d*) A reversal of (*c*). Many colours are used underneath and one colour placed on top.

Challenge 7

Using different brush movements and materials to produce different effects (dotting, fine work, deliberate production of different textures, thick paint and roughness, smooth gliding, etc.).

All of these challenges lead to patterning, free or regular, though some people react by painting a picture using whatever challenge is given. It is not suggested that this series is taken literally in order, nor that it gives an art education. It simply poses some ways of stimulating different uses of colour and, in schools, it will probably be used quite naturally as interspersed

Movement, colour and pattern

exercises, just as movement challenges are interspersed as the need arises between dances, and then used to enrich them.

Challenge 8

Ideas for the arrangement on the page may follow, precede or intersperse those for colour play, *e.g.*

(*a*) Start with colour from the centre, working outwards.

(*b*) Start from two centres placed in relation to each other; outside working in and so on (*see* Chapter 2).

Many teachers have found, particularly in primary schools, that the obvious freedom and link between movement, colour, sound, clay can influence the work in each other as an expressive form; *e.g.*, a movement session followed by painting or modelling, sound accompanying movement leading to a greater awareness of sound composition alone, words as a stimulus, patterns as a stimulus for group dance, and so on.

EXPERIMENTS WITH SHAPES

Similarly, guidance can be given in trying out shapes, and arrangements of shapes, as for colour play. Where necessary this can be as simple a challenge as cutting out one single shape, say a circle, and trying out how to place it on a page and what the different implications are. For instance:

The circle exactly in the centre gives an evenness and static arrangement.

The circle in the corner leaves an unbalanced area of space free (perhaps suitable for another shape).

Balanced use of remaining space areas.

Similarly work can be done with two shapes, three shapes, etc., and the teacher must be prepared to comment on the arrangements and say what each implication is.

Challenges to build shapes three-dimensionally can be with support beneath (like architectural building) or from above, *e.g.*, mobiles. These are very difficult to make to balance and work

Introduction to movement study and teaching

accurately and, although the balance could be worked out mathematically, I have always encouraged children to find out by trial and error. Various styles and types are possible: actual objects arranged; cut-out shapes, flat; shapes built out of material (boxes, etc.) and their relationships; materials which emphasise the space, especially the changing space formations, *e.g.*, concentric circles of wire.

Possibilities for group and partner work are obvious in group painting of murals, but I feel the main value of such work in colour and pattern is essentially individual, while one of the main contributions which dance and drama can make is in developing awareness of relationships through the group.

MAR 14 1994